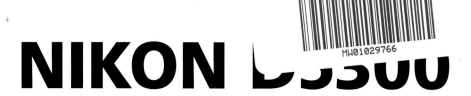

NIKON D5300

THE EXPANDED GUIDE

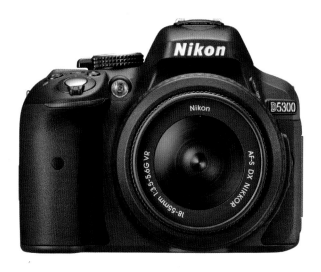

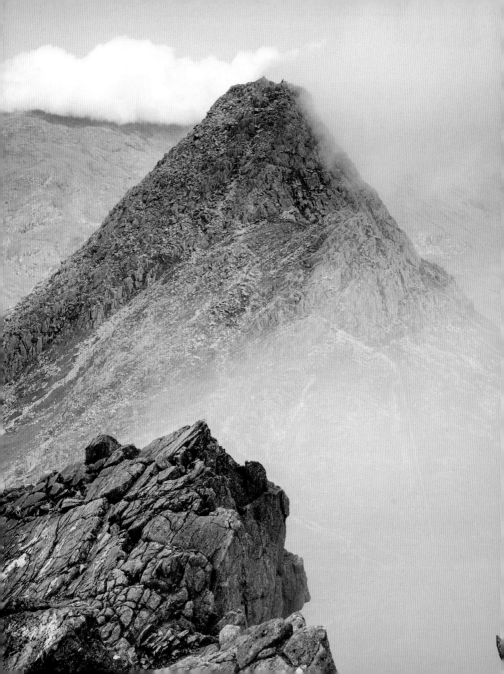

NIKON D5300
THE EXPANDED GUIDE

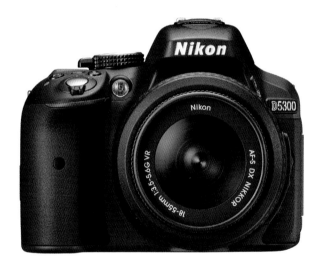

Jon Sparks

AMMONITE
PRESS

First published 2014 by
Ammonite Press
an imprint of AE Publications Ltd
166 High Street, Lewes, East Sussex, BN7 1XU, UK

ISBN 978-1-78145-096-3

British Library Cataloging in Publication Data: A catalog
record of this book is available from the British Library.

Editor: Rob Yarham
Series Editor: Richard Wiles
Design: Belkys Smock

Typefaces: Giacomo
Color reproduction by GMC Reprographics
Printed in China

‹‹ PAGE 2
PEAK PERFORMANCE
The Nikon D5300 is powerful
enough to take excellent
pictures, but small enough to
be carried almost anywhere.
30mm, 1/320 sec., f/9, ISO 200.

» CONTENTS

1 OVERVIEW

The D5300 is the latest model in Nikon's advanced "consumer" series, occupying a middle position in the DX-format camera range, between the entry-level D3200 and the "enthusiast" or "semi-pro" D7100. The D5XXX series stands apart from all other Nikon digital SLRs in having an articulating rear screen, which offers extra flexibility when shooting in Live View and can be especially helpful when shooting movies.

» EVOLUTION OF THE NIKON D5300

Nikon has always valued continuity as well as innovation; for instance, it has retained its tried and tested F lens-mount (originally introduced in 1959!). This means it's possible to use many classic Nikon lenses with the latest digital single-lens reflex cameras (DSLRs) like the D5300, though care is needed and some camera functions (e.g. autofocus) may be lost (see Chapter 7, *page 184*).

Nikon's first DSLR was the 1.3-megapixel E2s. It had no rear screen and images could only be viewed by connecting it to an

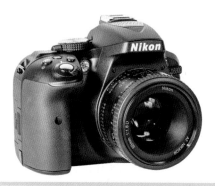

external device. A far more practical introduction was the 2.7-megapixel D1, in 1999. Still the most influential digital camera ever launched, the D1 was the first DSLR to approach the flexibility and ease of handling of 35mm SLRs. Its sensor adopted the DX format, subsequently used in every Nikon DSLR until the "full-frame" (FX) D3 in 2008.

In 2004, Nikon introduced their first "enthusiast" DSLR, the 6-megapixel D70; its direct descendants were the D80 (2006) and then the D90 (2008), but by then the range had diversified further, with a new "entry-level" series, beginning with the D40 (2006). This was followed by the D60 (2008) and then by the D3000, D3100, and D3200.

Meanwhile, the D90 was one of Nikon's most significant launches; a range of new features was overshadowed by one headline-grabber as it became the first DSLR capable of shooting video. The D90 remained on sale (and indeed is still listed today) even as many of its innovations

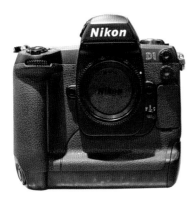

NIKON D1 (1999) ☆
The D1 was a revolutionary camera, making digital photography a practical, everyday proposition for thousands of professionals, not to mention amateur "early adopters".

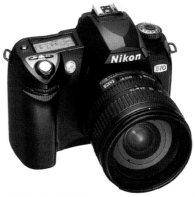

NIKON D70 (2004) ☆
The D70 was the camera which first persuaded a host of enthusiasts and not a few professionals (including the author) to take the plunge into digital photography.

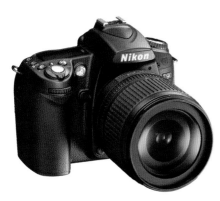

NIKON D90 (2008) ☆
The D90 had many new features, but one of these grabbed all the headlines as it became the first DSLR capable of shooting video.

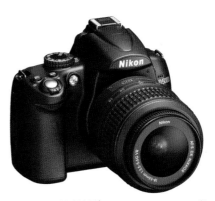

NIKON D5000 (2009) «
The D5300's predecessor brought an articulating screen, and established the basic design cues for the D5100, D5200, and D5300.

were incorporated into the D5000 (2009), which added a fold-out LCD screen. The D5100 (2011) had more pixels, a smaller overall form factor, and a repositioned screen pivot. The D5200 (early 2013) added refinements including a 24-megapixel sensor, enhanced image processing and an upgraded autofocus system.

And, less than a year later, along came the D5300—evolutionary rather than revolutionary, but still notable as Nikon's first DSLR with onboard WiFi and GPS.

SPORTING CHANCE   ❯❯
The D5300's up-to-date autofocus system can capture fast-moving subjects in low light, perfect for sports or wildlife photography.

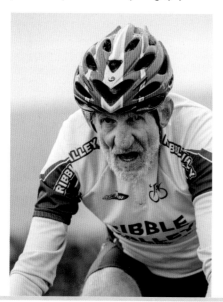

❯❯ ABOUT THE NIKON D5300

At first glance, the D5300 may look like a modest upgrade to the D5200, but there are several visible changes, and more hidden under the surface. The camera is a fraction smaller and lighter, thanks to the use of innovative carbon-fiber-reinforced thermoplastics for structural elements of the body, while the rear screen is slightly larger than that of its predecessors at 3.2in. (80mm).

The D5300 has a 24-megapixel sensor —the same as the D5200—but there's a major difference as the D5300 has dispensed with an "anti-aliasing" (AA) filter in front of its sensor—the first Nikon to do away with the AA filter was the D800e. This should make images even sharper, and results seem to bear this out, but you will only see the difference with good lenses and technique. The D5300 also uses the latest EXPEED 4 image processing system.

Two other significant innovations on the D5300 are the introduction of WiFi and GPS capabilities. The camera is not only smaller and lighter than its predecessor, but has better power management, with battery life notably better than the D5200.

Like all Nikon SLRs the D5300 is part of a vast system of lenses, accessories, and software. This *Expanded Guide* to the Nikon D5300 will guide you through all aspects of the camera's operation, and its relation to the system as a whole.

» NIKON DX-FORMAT SENSOR

DX-format sensors, measuring approximately 23.6 x 15.8mm (with slight variations), have been used in every Nikon DSLR from the D1 onward, until the arrival of "full-frame" FX-format cameras (e.g. D4, D800, D610). The sensors in these models are approximately 36 x 24mm.

The number of pixels on the sensor has risen from 2.7 million on the D1 to around 24 million across the current DX range. Early models used CCD sensors, but today CMOS (Complementary Metal Oxide Semiconductor) sensors are used in all of Nikon's DSLRs.

The DX format dictates a 1.5x magnification factor, relative to the same lenses used on 35mm and FX cameras. The D5300's CMOS sensor measures 23.5 x 15.6 mm, making it fractionally smaller than some other models, though there's no real significance in this. Its 24 million pixels produce images at a native size of 6000 x 4000 pixels,

making them suitable for demanding large prints and book and magazine reproduction. Dispensing with an anti-aliasing (optical low-pass) filter helps sharpness still further.

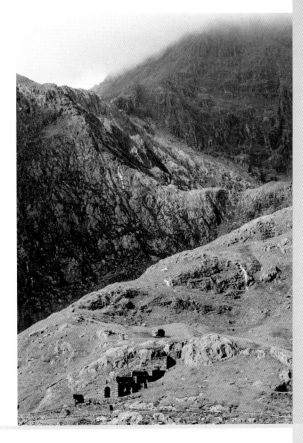

SHARP SHOOTING   »
The lack of an anti-aliasing filter enhances the sharpness of the D5300's images, especially with good lenses and technique.

» MAIN FEATURES

Sensor

Sensor 24.2 effective megapixel DX-format RGB CMOS sensor measuring 23.5 x 15.6mm and producing maximum image size of 6000 × 4000 pixels; self-cleaning function. No optical low-pass (anti-aliasing) filter.

Image processor

EXPEED 4 image processing system featuring 14-bit analog-to-digital (A/D) conversion with 16-bit image processing.

Focus

39-point autofocus system, supported by Nikon Scene Recognition System, which tracks subjects by shape, position, and color. Three focus modes: (S) Single-servo AF; (C) Continuous-servo AF; and (M) Manual focus. Three AF-area modes: Single-area AF; Dynamic-area AF with option of 3D tracking; and Auto-area AF. Rapid focus point selection and focus lock.

ISO range

Between 100 and 12,800, with extensions (Hi) up to 25,600. Exposure compensation between −5 Ev and +5 Ev; exposure lock and exposure bracketing facility.

Exposure modes

Two fully auto modes: auto; auto (flash off). 16 Scene modes: Portrait; Landscape; Child; Sports; Close up; Night portrait; Night landscape; Party/indoor; Beach/snow; Sunset; Dusk/dawn; Pet portrait; Candlelight; Blossom; Autumn colors; Food. Nine Effects modes: Night Vision; Color Sketch; Miniature Effect; Selective Color; Silhouette; High key; Low key; Toy camera effect; HDR painting. Four user-controlled modes: (P) Programmed auto with flexible program; (A) Aperture-priority auto; (S) Shutter-priority auto; (M) Manual.

Shutter

Shutter speeds from 1/4000 sec. to 30 sec., plus B (bulb). Maximum continuous frame advance 5fps. Quiet mode, self-timer, remote control, and mirror-up modes.

Viewfinder

Pentamirror viewfinder with 95% coverage and 0.82x magnification.

LCD monitor

Vari-angle 3.2in. (81mm), 1037k-dot TFT LCD display with 100% frame coverage.

Movie mode
Movie capture in .MOV format (Motion-JPEG compression) with image size (pixels) of: 1920 x 1280; 1280 x 720; 640 x 424.

Buffer
Buffer capacity allows up to 100 frames (JPEG fine, large) to be captured in a continuous burst at 5fps, or approximately 15 RAW files.

Built-in flash
Pop-up flash (manually activated) with Guide Number of 12 (m) or 39 (ft) at ISO 100 supports i-TTL balanced fill-flash for DSLR (when matrix or center- weighted metering is selected) and Standard i-TTL flash for DSLR (when spot metering is selected). Up to 10 flash-sync modes (dependent on exposure mode in use): Auto; auto + red-eye reduction; auto slow sync; auto slow sync + red-eye reduction; fill-flash; slow sync; rear-curtain sync; rear-curtain slow sync; red-eye reduction; slow sync + red-eye reduction. Flash compensation from −3 to +1 Ev.

Custom functions
22 parameters and elements of the camera's operations can be customized through the Custom Setting menu.

File formats
The D5300 supports NEF (RAW) (14-bit) and JPEG (Fine/Normal/Basic) file formats plus .MOV movie format.

Storage
Secure Digital (SD) card slot; accepts SDHC and SDXC cards.

System back-up
Compatible with around 60 current and many non-current Nikkor lenses (functionality varies with older lenses); SB-series flashguns; Wireless Remote Control ML-L3 and WR-R10; ME-1 stereo microphone; and many more Nikon system accessories.

Connectivity
Onboard WiFi and GPS. Connectors for external microphone, USB/AV, HDMI, and Nikon remote cords/wireless controllers.

Software
Supplied with Nikon View NX2 (incorporates Nikon Transfer 2); compatible with Nikon Capture NX2 and many third-party imaging applications.

1 » FULL FEATURES & CAMERA LAYOUT

FRONT OF CAMERA

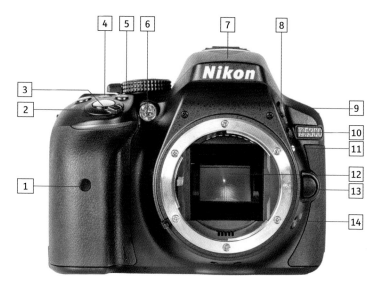

1	Infrared receiver (front)	**8**	Flash/Flash mode/
2	Power switch		Flash compensation button
3	Shutter-release button	**9**	Camera strap mount
4	Live View switch	**10**	Fn button
5	Mode Dial	**11**	Mounting mark
6	AF-assist illuminator/Self-timer/	**12**	Mirror
	Red-eye reduction lamp	**13**	Lens-release button
7	Built-in flash	**14**	Lens mount

BACK OF CAMERA

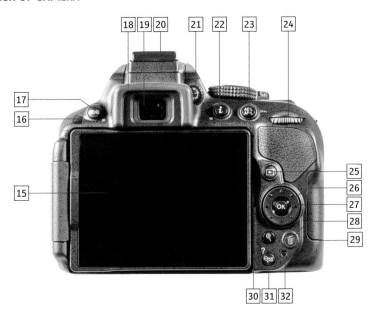

15 Monitor	**25** Playback button
16 Infrared receiver (rear)	**26** Multi-selector
17 MENU button	**27** OK button
18 Eyecup	**28** Delete button
19 Viewfinder eyepiece	**29** Memory card slot cover
20 Accessory hotshoe cover	**30** Playback zoom in button
21 Diopter adjustment dial	**31** Thumbnail/ playback zoom out/ Help button
22 Information edit button	
23 AE-L/AF-L/Protect button	**32** Memory card access lamp
24 Command Dial	

1 » FULL FEATURES & CAMERA LAYOUT

TOP OF CAMERA

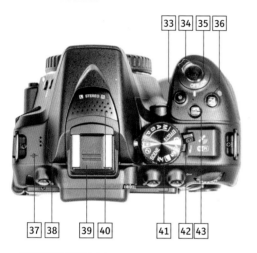

LEFT SIDE

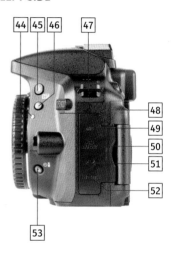

33	Movie-record button
34	Power switch
35	Shutter-release button
36	Exposure compensation/ Aperture adjustment/ Flash compensation button
37	Focal plane mark
38	Speaker
39	Accessory hotshoe
40	Stereo microphone
41	Mode Dial
42	Live View switch
43	INFO button

44	Mounting mark
45	Flash/Flash mode/Flash compensation button
46	Fn button
47	Camera strap mount
48	USB and AV connector
49	External microphone connector
50	Connector cover
51	Accessory terminal
52	HDMI mini-pin connector
53	Release Mode/Self-timer/ Remote control

BOTTOM OF CAMERA

RIGHT SIDE

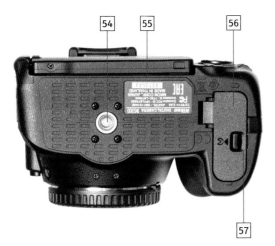

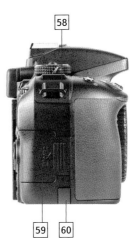

54 Tripod socket (¼in.)

55 Camera serial number

56 Battery compartment

57 Battery compartment release lever

58 Camera strap mount

59 Memory card slot cover

60 Power connector cover for optional power connector

1 » INFORMATION DISPLAY

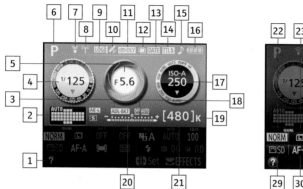
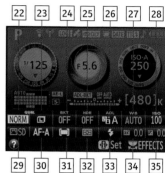

1	Help icon	19	"K" (when over 1000 exposures remain)
2	Auto-area AF indicator	20	Exposure/Exposure compensation/ Bracketing progress indicator
3	Bracketing indicator		
4	Shutter speed	21	Exposures remaining/White balance recording/Capture mode indicator
5	Aperture (f-number)		
6	Shooting mode	22	Image quality
7	Eye-Fi connection indicator	23	Image size
8	WiFi connection indicator	24	Bracketing indicator
9	Track log indicator	25	HDR indicator
10	Satellite signal indicator	26	Active D-Lighting
11	Exposure delay mode	27	White balance
12	Multiple exposure indicator	28	ISO sensitivity
13	Print date indicator	29	Picture control
14	Flash control indicator	30	Focus mode
15	"Beep" indicator	31	AF-area mode
16	Battery indicator	32	Metering
17	ISO sensitivity	33	Flash mode
18	ADL bracketing amount	34	Flash compensation
		35	Exposure compensation

» VIEWFINDER DISPLAY

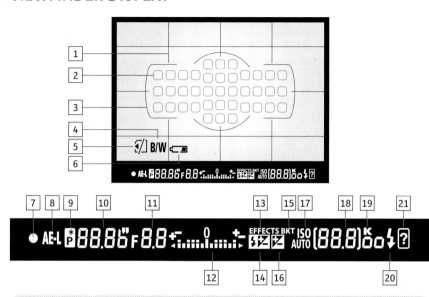

1 Framing grid	13 Special effects mode indicator
2 Focus points	14 Flash compensation indicator
3 AF area brackets	15 Bracketing indicator
4 Monochrome indicator	16 Exposure compensation indicator
5 No memory card warning	17 Auto ISO sensitivity indicator
6 Low battery warning	18 Number of exposures remaining/
7 Focus indicator	Number of exposures remaining in
8 AE lock indicator	buffer/white balance recording
9 Flexible program indicator	indicator/exposure compensation
10 Shutter speed	value/flash compensation value/
11 Aperture	ISO sensitivity/Capture mode indicator
12 Exposure indicator/exposure	19 K (when over 1000 exposures remain)
compensation display/electronic	20 Flash-ready indicator
rangefinder	21 Warning indicator

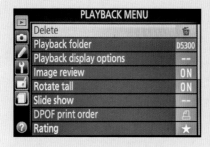

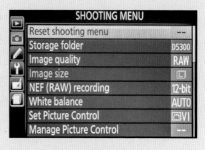

Playback menu
> Delete
> Playback folder
> Playback display options
> Image review
> Rotate tall
> Slide show
> DPOF Print order
> Rating
> Select to send to smart device

Shooting menu
> Reset shooting menu
> Storage folder
> Image quality
> Image size
> NEF (RAW) recording
> White balance
> Set Picture Control
> Manage Picture Control
> Auto distortion control
> Color space
> Active D-Lighting
> HDR (high dynamic range)
> Long exposure NR
> High ISO NR
> ISO sensitivity settings
> Release mode
> Multiple exposure
> Interval timer shooting
> Movie settings

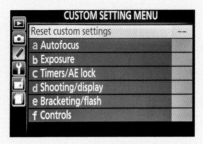

Custom Setting menu
> Reset custom settings

a: Autofocus
> a1 AF-C priority selectiona2
> Number of focus points
> a3 Built-in AF-assist illuminator
> a4 Rangefinder

b: Exposure
> b1 Ev steps for exposure control

c: Timers/AE Lock
> c1 Shutter-release button AE-L
> c2 Auto off timers
> c3 Self-timer
> c4 Remote on duration (ML-L3)

d: Shooting/display
> d1 Beep
> d2 Viewfinder grid display
> d3 ISO display
> d4 File number sequence
> d5 Exposure delay mode
> d6 Print date

e: Bracketing/flash
> e1 Flash cntrl for built-in flash
> e2 Auto bracketing set

f: Controls
> f1 Assign Fn button
> f2 Assign *AE-L/AF-L* button
> f3 Reverse dial rotation
> f4 Slot empty release lock
> f5 Reverse indicators

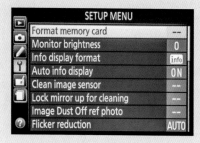

Setup menu
> Format memory card
> Monitor brightness
> Info display format
> Auto info display
> Clean image sensor
> Lock mirror up for cleaning
> Image Dust Off ref photo
> Flicker reduction
> Time zone and date
> Language
> Auto image rotation
> Image comment
> Location data
> Video mode
> HDMI
> Remote control
> Wi-Fi
> Eye-Fi upload
> Conformity marking
> Firmware version

Retouch menu
> D-Lighting
> Red-eye correction
> Trim
> Monochrome
> Filter effects
> Color balance
> Image overlay
> NEF (RAW) processing
> Resize
> Quick retouch
> Straighten
> Distortion control
> Fisheye
> Color outline
> Color sketch
> Perspective control
> Miniature effect
> Selective color
> Edit movie
> Side-by-side comparison

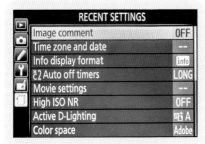

RECENT SETTINGS	
Image comment	OFF
Time zone and date	--
Info display format	info
⏱2 Auto off timers	LONG
Movie settings	--
High ISO NR	OFF
Active D-Lighting	醯 A
Color space	Adobe

My Menu/Recent Settings
> Add items
> Remove items
> Rank items
> Choose tab

2 FUNCTIONS

The Nikon D5300 sports over a dozen control buttons, a Mode Dial, a Command Dial, and a Multi-selector, so it may appear complex and daunting to users familiar with digital compacts. However, this complexity is a sign of the power that it offers. You can do a heck of a lot with this camera.

Also, this apparent complexity arises because so much of the camera's power is on the surface. You can access most key functions rapidly through the buttons and dials, without having to delve into menus. Ultimately, this is beneficial. Cameras which make you use menus for most settings are slower and more cumbersome in operation, and may discourage you from exploration and discovery.

Still, the D5300 can also be as simple to use as any "point-and-shoot" camera,

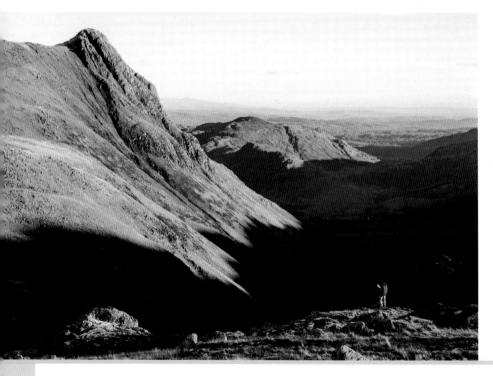

while still delivering far superior image quality. It will be set to its Full Auto mode when you first unpack it, and at any time you can revert to full auto operation by setting the Mode Dial to the 🗖 position. You can also quickly reset all other camera settings to the initial factory default by holding down the **MENU** and 🖽 buttons (marked with green dots) together for at least 2 seconds.

However, the D5300 offers much greater creative control than most compact cameras. Its design allows you to make a gradual transition from leaving everything to the camera to taking full control of its key functions.

Tip

The printed manual supplied with the camera is a cut-down version: a more comprehensive Nikon Reference Manual *is provided on CD, and can also be downloaded from Nikon websites.*

FAMILIARIZATION   «
When you unpack a new camera, it's tempting to start shooting right away—and taking pictures is the best way to learn. However, it still makes sense to peruse this book first, to ensure you don't miss out on new features and functions. *42mm, 1/125 sec., f/10, ISO 100.*

Leaving the camera at default settings misses out on much of its imaging power, and the intention of this chapter is to provide a step-by-step introduction to its most important features and functions. Even in a much longer book it would be impossible to fully explore every last detail, so we'll concentrate on these aspects which will be relevant to the majority of photographers.

Tip

The camera also provides on-screen help during shooting and when using the menus. Press 🔍🖿 to bring up information relating to the item currently selected on the screen. You can't access Help during playback as the button then has a different function.

ON-SCREEN HELP   ❯

> **?** Auto image rotation
>
> Record camera orientation when taking photographs.
> Images taken when "Off" is selected will not be rotated for display during playback.

2 » CAMERA PREPARATION

Some basic operations, like charging the battery and inserting a memory card, are essential before the camera can be used. When first switched on, the camera will also prompt you to set language, time, date, and time zone—see Setup menu in Chapter 3, *page 122.*

› Attaching the strap

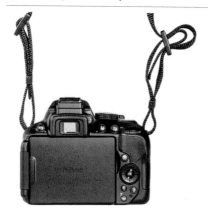

ATTACHING THE STRAP
The strap is shown fully tightened on the left, threaded but not yet tightened on the right.

To attach the supplied strap, ensure the padded side faces inwards (so the maker's name faces out). Attach either end to the appropriate eyelet, located at top left and right sides of the camera. Loosen the strap where it runs through the buckle, then pass the end of the strap through the eyelet and back through the buckle. Bring the end of the strap back through the buckle, under the first length of strap already threaded (see photo). Repeat on the other side. Adjust the length as required, but ensure a good "tail" (minimum 2in. or 50mm) extends beyond each buckle for security. Tighten the strap to seat it snugly within the buckle.

> **Note:**
> This method is different from that shown in the Nikon Reference Manual, but is both more secure and neater.

› Adjusting for eyesight

The D5300 offers dioptric adjustment, between −1.7 and +1 m^{-1}, to allow for individual variations in eyesight. Make sure this is optimized for your eyesight (with glasses or contact lenses if you normally use them). The diopter adjustment dial is by the top right corner of the Viewfinder. With the camera switched on, rotate the dial until the Viewfinder readouts appear sharpest (don't use the image in the Viewfinder itself for this).

Unless your eyesight changes, you

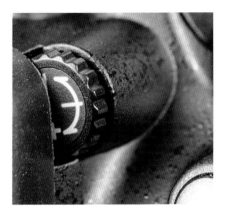

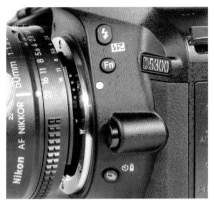

DIOPTER ADJUSTMENT ⌃
The diopter adjustment dial enables you to
correct the Viewfinder for your eyesight.

should only need to do this once.
Supplementary Viewfinder lenses are
available if this adjustment proves
insufficient.

› Mounting lenses

The ability to use a wide range of lenses
(see Chapter 7, *page 184*) is one of the
great advantages of a DSLR.
  Switch the camera off before changing
lenses. Remove the rear lens cap and the
camera body cap (or the lens already
mounted). To remove a lens, press the
lens-release button and turn the lens
clockwise (as you face the front of the
camera). Align the index mark on the lens

MOUNTING LENSES ⌃
One of the advantages of a DSLR is the ability to
fit a wide range of different lenses.

with the one on the camera body (white
dot), insert the lens into the camera and
turn it anti-clockwise until it clicks home.
Do not use force; if the lens is correctly
aligned it will mount smoothly.

Warning!

Avoid touching the electrical contacts
on lens and camera body, as dirty
contacts can cause malfunctions.
Replace lenses or body caps as soon
as possible.

See Chapter 7 Lenses (*page 184*) for
information on compatible lenses; the
Nikon Reference Manual has further detail.

2

› Inserting and removing memory cards

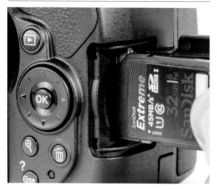

INSERTING A MEMORY CARD ⌃
The D5300 stores images on Secure Digital (SD) cards, including SDHC and SDXC cards.

To store photographs, you'll need to insert a memory card (*see page 205*).

1) Switch off the camera. Check that the access lamp on the camera back (below the Multi-selector) is off.

2) Slide the card slot cover (right side of the camera) to the rear. It will spring open.

3) To remove a memory card, press the card gently into its slot; it will spring out slightly, allowing you to remove it.

4) Insert a card with its label facing the rear and the terminals along the card edge facing into the slot. The "cut-off" corner of the card will be at the top. Gently push the card into the slot until it clicks home. The green access lamp will light briefly.

5) Close the card slot cover.

› Formatting a memory card

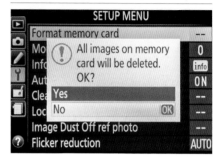

FORMATTING A MEMORY CARD ⌃

You'll need to format new memory cards, or ones that have been used in another camera, before using them with the D5300. Formatting is also the most efficient way to erase images from a card so you can reuse it, but make sure they are saved elsewhere.

To format a memory card
1) Press **MENU** and select the Setup menu from the symbols at left of the screen.

2) Select **Format memory** card and press ⊛.

3) Select **Yes** and press ⊛.

› Battery

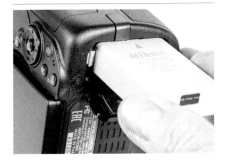

INSERTING THE BATTERY ⌃

The Nikon D5300 is supplied with an EN-EL14a li-ion rechargeable battery.

Inserting and removing the battery

Turn the camera upside down and locate the battery compartment, below the handgrip. Release the latch to open the compartment. Insert the battery, contacts first, with the face that says "Nikon" facing away from the lens. Use the battery to nudge the gold-colored latch aside, then slide the battery gently in until the latch clicks home. Close the battery compartment cover, making sure that it clicks shut and is secure.

To remove the battery, you must switch off the camera first, and then open the compartment cover. Press the gold latch to release the battery and pull it gently out of the compartment.

Charging the battery

Use the supplied MH-24 charger to charge the battery. Remove the battery terminal cover (if attached) and insert the battery into the charger with the maker's name uppermost and terminals facing the contacts on the charger. Press the battery gently but firmly into position. Plug the charger into a mains outlet. The charge lamp blinks while the battery is charging, then shines steadily when charging is complete. A completely flat battery will take around 90 minutes to recharge fully.

Battery life

Under standard test conditions (CIPA) the D5300 should deliver around 600 shots before the battery needs recharging; however, this can vary widely depending on how you use the camera. If you hardly use the LCD screen, i.e. rarely changing settings or reviewing your shots, you may achieve several times this number. On the other hand, heavy screen use, such as extensive Live View shooting, can drastically reduce it, as can heavy use of the built-in flash.

Battery life may also be significantly shorter if you're shooting in temperatures below 0°C (see Chapter 8, *page 218*).

The battery icon in the Information Display shows roughly how much charge remains. The icon blinks when the battery is exhausted, and a low battery warning also appears in the Viewfinder.

2 » BASIC OPERATION

With strap, lens, battery, and memory card on board, the D5300 is ready to shoot. The camera arrives set to Auto mode and with its LCD screen stowed away. The D5300 will happily shoot indefinitely like this, but as soon as you want to change any settings, review, or playback your shots, use Live View, or shoot movies, you'll need to use the screen and its Information Display (see below).

As you begin to explore a wider range of options, the key controls are the Mode Dial, Command Dial, and Multi-selector, along with the Release mode button. However, in Auto and Scene modes it is perfectly possible (though not necessarily recommended) to shoot with virtually no recourse to any of these.

› Switching the camera on

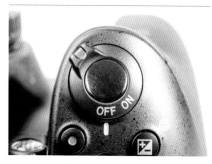

POWER SWITCH AND SHUTTER-RELEASE BUTTON ⌃

The power switch surrounds the shutter-release button. It has two self-explanatory settings: OFF and ON.

> **Tip**
>
> *If the power switch is turned OFF while the camera is recording image(s), the camera will finish the process before turning off.*

› Using the LCD screen

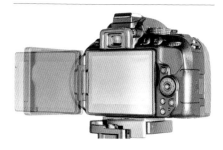

A RANGE OF SCREEN POSITIONS ⌃

To use the screen, grasp the tabs at top right and bottom right and ease it away from the camera. The screen can be angled and rotated to a wide range of positions but is more vulnerable when opened out. For normal use, open the screen out, rotate it 180° (push the top away from you) then fold it back against the camera body until it clicks into place. It's obviously convenient to leave the screen in this position, but it is open to scratches and other damage. It's safer to stow the screen away when transporting or storing the camera; if you set a suitable Shooting mode beforehand, you can grab shots quickly without needing to open out the screen first.

Tip

The screen can be hard to see clearly in bright sunlight. Screen shades are available which help to get around this problem (see page 213).

› Operating the shutter

The shutter-release button operates in two stages. Pressing it lightly, until you feel initial resistance, activates the metering and focus functions. Half-pressure also clears the Information Display, menus, or image playback, making the D5300 instantly ready to shoot. Press the button more firmly (but still smoothly) to take the picture.

› Information Display

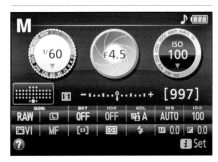

INFORMATION DISPLAY— GRAPHIC FORMAT ⌃

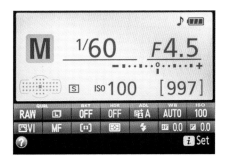

INFORMATION DISPLAY— CLASSIC FORMAT ⌃

The Information Display is central to using the D5300. To activate it, do any of these:
– Half-press and release the shutter-release button (if you maintain pressure the information display will not appear);
– Press **INFO** on top of the camera;
– Press ◄🔘► on the rear of the camera.

This brings up a display showing the selected exposure mode, the aperture, shutter speed, and a range of other detail.

This screen can be displayed in either of two formats. **Graphic** format, active by default, uses icons and pictures to illustrate the effect of various settings. **Classic** format presents the information traditionally, using text and numbers. The color scheme can also be changed. These options are exercised through the Setup menu (*page 122*).

the various settings. To make changes, press ⓞⓚ, and the range of options for that setting appears. Use the Multi-selector to move through these options; when the one you want is highlighted, press ⓞⓚ again to select it.

> **Note:**
> We've coined the term "Active Information Display". It is not used in Nikon's own manual, which instead refers clunkily to "placing the cursor in the Information Display".

› Active Information Display

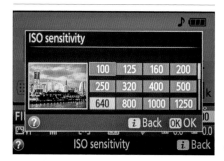

THE ACTIVE INFORMATION DISPLAY SHOWING ISO SENSITIVITY OPTIONS ⌃

The initial Information Display is passive, i.e. it displays many settings but does not allow you to change them. To make changes possible, press ◀▤▶ while the initial display is visible (if the screen is blank, press the button twice). The lower panel on the screen is highlighted and you can use the Multi-selector to move through

› Mode Dial

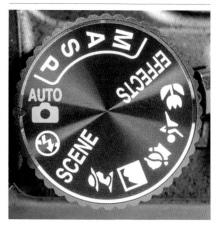

The Mode setting, chosen from this dial, determines whether the camera operates entirely automatically or requires some level of input from you. It has 13 positions, split into four groups: Full Auto modes, User-control modes, Scene modes and Effects. For a full run-down of these see under Exposure modes, *page 34*.

> ## Warning!
>
> **The Mode Dial does not have a lock. It is firmly click-stopped, so accidental shifts are rare, but they can occur.**

› Command Dial

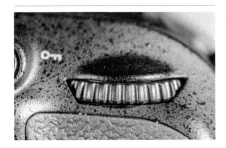

THE COMMAND DIAL ⌃

The Command Dial falls naturally under the right thumb when the camera is in shooting position. It is fundamental to the operation of the Nikon D5300, especially in the user-control modes.

› Operating the Command Dial

The dial's function is flexible, varying according to the operating mode at the time. In Shutter-priority (S) or Manual (M) mode, rotating the Command Dial selects

the shutter speed. In Aperture-priority (A) mode it selects the aperture. In Program (P) mode it engages flexible program, changing the combination of shutter speed and aperture. For descriptions of these modes *see page 53*.

The Command Dial is also used to select from among the more specialized Scene or Effects modes when the Mode Dial is set to SCENE or EFFECTS. When shooting in ▲ and ⚡ modes, the Command Dial has no direct effect.

› Multi-selector

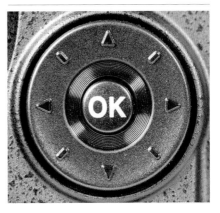

THE MULTI-SELECTOR ⌃

The other principal control is the Multi-selector. Its main use when shooting pictures is to select and change settings in the Active Information Display; the ⊙ button at its center is used to confirm settings. The Multi-selector is also used for navigating through the menus, and through images on playback. These uses will be covered in the relevant sections.

› Release mode

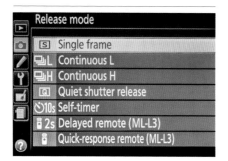

SETTING RELEASE MODE ⌃

"Release mode" may seem an obscure term. It determines whether the camera takes a single picture or shoots continuously. It can also allow you to delay the shot or trigger the camera remotely.

1) Press ⃟ to bring up a list of options (see table below).

2) Release ⃟; until you do so, you can't do anything with the options.

3) Highlight the desired option and press ⃝ to make it active. The chosen release mode is shown in the Information Display.

Seven possible release modes can be selected in this way.

› Buffer

Images are initially stored in the camera's internal memory ("buffer") before being written to the memory card. The maximum number of images that can be recorded in a continuous burst depends upon file quality, release mode, memory card capacity, and how much buffer space is available. The figure for the number of burst frames possible at current settings is shown in the Viewfinder at bottom right when the shutter-release button is half-depressed. e.g. **[r05]**.

If **(0)** appears, the buffer is full, and no more shots will be taken until enough data has been transferred to the memory card to free up space in the buffer. This normally happens very quickly, but if you're shooting in ⃟L or ⃟H Continuous modes you may notice a slow-down or a break in the rhythm of the shutter.

> **Note:**
> In theory you can shoot up to 100 shots continuously at 5fps, but this is probably only possible when image quality is set to **Basic**. When it's **Fine**, I've never managed more than about 20 shots without some signs of slowdown; in **Raw**, about 8. This is with a 45Mb/sec. memory card.

RELEASE MODE OPTIONS

Setting	Description
S Single	The camera takes a single shot each time the shutter release is fully depressed.
⤴L Continuous L	The camera fires continuously as long as the shutter release is fully depressed. The maximum frame rate is 3fps.
⤴H Continuous H	The camera fires continuously as long as the shutter release is fully depressed. The maximum frame rate is 5fps.
Q Quiet shutter release	Similar to Single Frame, but mirror remains up and shutter does not re-cock until shutter-release button is released, making operation quieter (but by no means silent).
⟳ Self-timer	The shutter is released a set interval after the release button is depressed. Can be used to minimize camera shake and for self-portraits. The default interval is 10 sec., but 2 sec., 5 sec., or 20 sec. can be set using Custom Setting c3. Up to nine shots can be taken for each release. Camera resets to S after each release.
⊟ 2s Delayed remote	Requires the optional ML-L3 remote control; shutter fires approximately 2 sec. after remote is tripped. Camera resets to S if remote is not used within a certain time (set by Custom setting c4) slap," but now superseded in many situations by Live View mode.
⊟ Quick response remote	Requires the optional ML-L3 remote control; shutter fires immediately when remote is tripped. Camera resets to S if remote is not used within a certain time (set by Custom setting c4).

You can select Release modes no matter what Exposure mode is active, but whenever you switch to any Auto, Scene, or Effects mode, the camera reverts to the default Release mode for that Exposure mode (usually S).

2 » EXPOSURE MODES

The choice of exposure mode makes a significant difference to the amount of control you can—or can't—exercise. Exposure modes are selected from the Mode Dial, with the addition of the Command Dial for some more specialized modes. The D5300 has a very wide choice of Exposure modes, but they fall conveniently into three main groups: Full Auto modes, Scene modes, and User-control modes. There's also an EFFECTS position on the Mode Dial for more extreme or wacky results.

In Auto modes and Scene modes the majority of settings are controlled by the camera. These go beyond basic shooting settings (shutter speed and aperture) to include options such as release mode, whether or not flash can be used, and how the camera processes the shot. The difference is that Full Auto modes use compromise settings to cover most eventualities while Scene mode settings are tailored to particular shooting situations.

User-control modes, by contrast, give you complete freedom to control virtually everything on the camera.

KITE SURFER   ❯❯
The D5300 is able to tackle a very wide range of subjects and lighting conditions. *160mm, 1/2000 sec., f/6.3, ISO 200.*

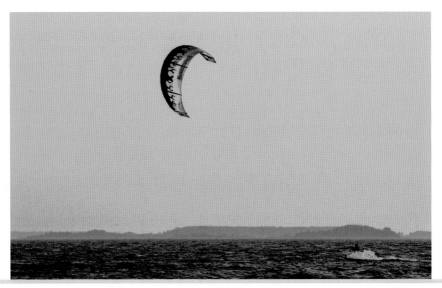

Mode group	Exposure mode	
Full Auto modes	AUTO Auto Auto (flash off)	Leave all decisions about settings to the camera.
Scene modes (Directly selectable on Mode Dial)	Portrait Landscape Child Sports Close-up	Choose the Scene mode to suit the subject and the camera then employs appropriate settings.
Scene modes (Set the Mode Dial to **SCENE** and use Information Display/ Command Dial)	Night portrait Night landscape Party/indoor Beach/snow Sunset Dusk/dawn Pet portrait Candlelight Blossom Autumn colors Food	
Special Effects (Set the Mode Dial to **EFFECTS** and use Information Display/ Command Dial)	Night Vision Color Sketch Toy Camera Effect Miniature Effect Selective Color Silhouette High key Low key	Use for more extreme pictorial effects.
User-control modes	P Program S Shutter-priority A Aperture-priority M Manual	Allow control over the full range of camera settings.

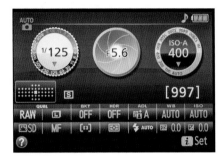

FULL AUTO MODE   ⌃

Nikon calls these "point-and-shoot" modes, which is probably a fair reflection of the kind of photography for which they're likely to be used. They work pretty well, most of the time; you'll hardly ever get a shot that doesn't "come out" at all, but you will sometimes find that the results aren't exactly what you were aiming for. After all, in these modes the camera, not you, decides what kind of picture you are taking and how it should look.

There's only one difference between these two modes. In ⬛ Auto mode the built-in flash will pop up automatically if the camera determines light levels are too low, and can only be turned off via the Active Information Display (*see page 30*). (If a separate accessory flashgun is attached and switched on, this overrides the built-in unit.)

In ⬦ Auto (flash off) mode the flash stays off no matter what. This is useful whenever flash is banned or would be intrusive, or when you just want to discover what the D5300 can do in low light.

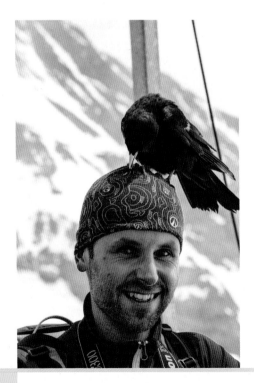

FULL AUTO MODE   «
Full auto mode is ideal for situations when shots need to be grabbed quickly. *110mm, 1/250 sec., f/11, ISO 200.*

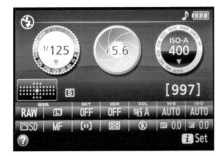

AUTO (FLASH OFF) MODE   ⌃

Taking the picture

Basic picture taking is essentially the same in all Full Auto and Scene modes.

1) Select the desired mode.

2) Frame the picture.

3) Half-depress the release button to activate focusing and exposure. The focus point(s) will be displayed in the Viewfinder image, and shutter speed and aperture settings will appear at the bottom of the Viewfinder.

4) Fully depress the shutter release to take the picture.

AUTO (FLASH OFF) MODE   »
Auto (flash off) mode is useful for when flash might be disruptive or annoying, or where it would destroy a mood. *120mm, 1/125 sec., f/4, ISO 3200.*

› Exposure warnings

If the camera detects that light levels are too low or too high for an acceptable exposure, warnings will be displayed. The Viewfinder display blinks, and in the Information Display you'll see a flashing question mark and a warning message. The camera will still take pictures, but results may be unsatisfactory; for instance, if it's too dark, shots may be underexposed or subject to camera shake. However, the warning can still appear even when the camera is on a tripod.

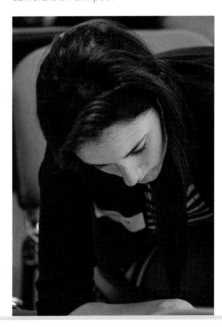

» SCENE MODES

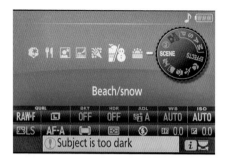

VIRTUAL MODE DIAL
A "virtual Mode Dial" appears briefly when you first set the Mode Dial to SCENE.

Scene modes are designed to tailor camera settings to specific subjects and conditions. Seasoned photographers may disdain them, as they take many decisions out of your hands. However, even the most experienced may find them handy on occasion, as a quick way to set the camera for shooting a particular kind of image. If you're less experienced, you will find that Scene modes are a good way to discover how differently the camera can interpret the same subject. This makes them a great stepping stone to the full range of options offered by the D5300. The first step is to understand how the various Scene modes work and to be aware of the difference they can make in your images: an obvious way to do this is to shoot the same subject using different modes.

Scene modes control basic shooting parameters such as how the camera focuses and how it sets shutter speed and aperture. They also determine how the image is processed by the camera (assuming you are shooting JPEG images, see page 78). For instance, Nikon Picture Controls (page 99) are predetermined. In ♥ Portrait mode, for example, the camera applies a Portrait Picture Control, which gives natural color rendition and is particularly kind to skin tones. Most Scene modes also employ Auto White Balance (see page 80), but in a few cases the White Balance setting is predetermined to suit specific subjects.

Five Scene modes are directly selectable using the Mode Dial; eleven more are selected by first setting the Mode Dial to **SCENE**, then rotating the Command Dial. The Information Display activates and then, as you rotate the Command Dial, the display cycles through the eleven modes. For each one, a thumbnail image gives an example of an appropriate subject and the way it should turn out when this mode is used. The selection disappears after a few seconds; turn the Command Dial again when you need to reactivate it.

› 🏃 Portrait

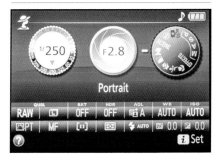

› 🏃 Child

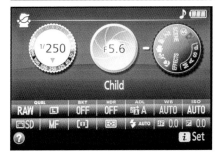

In Portrait mode the camera sets a relatively wide aperture to reduce depth of field (*page 60*), helping subjects stand out from their background. The camera also selects the focus point automatically, using Face Detection, although you can select other focusing options. The flash pops up if the camera determines light levels are too low, but can (and often should) be turned off via the Active Information Display. Attaching a separate flashgun will override the built-in-flash—and usually improves results (*see page 148*).

Child mode is similar to Portrait mode, but one difference is that the camera tends to set higher shutter speeds, because children are less likely than adults to sit still. JPEG processing is based on a Standard Picture Control rather than Portrait for results that are more vivid overall, with pleasing skin tones. The flash activates automatically, but its limitations are just as noticeable as in 🏃 Portrait. It can be turned off via the Active Information Display.

CHILD MODE ⌄
Child mode is tailored to more active subjects. *200mm, 1/250 sec., f/5.6, ISO 320.*

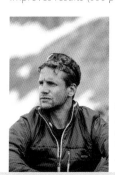

PORTRAIT MODE «
Portrait mode restricts depth of field in the image. *135mm, 1/250 sec., f/5.6, ISO 200.*

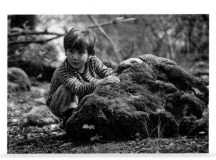

2 › 🏔 Landscape

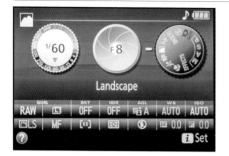

side, so a tripod is often advisable. The camera also selects the focus point automatically, though this can be overridden. A Landscape Picture Control is applied to give vibrant colors. The built-in flash remains off, even in low light, and you can't activate it manually. However, you can use a separate flashgun.

In Landscape mode, the camera sets a small aperture, aiming to maximize depth of field (*page 60*). Small apertures mean that shutter speeds can be on the slow

LANDSCAPE MODE ⌄

Landscape mode should ensure images with vibrant colors and good depth of field. *18mm, 1/100 sec., f/10, ISO 100.*

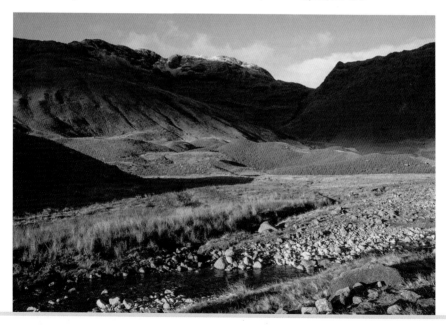

› ⚡ Sports

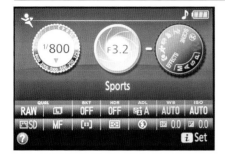

Sports mode is suited to shooting not just sports but other fast-moving subjects, including wildlife. The camera will set a fast shutter speed to freeze the action. This usually implies a wide aperture and therefore shallow depth of field. The camera initially selects the central focus point, but if it detects subject movement it will track it using all 39 focus points. You can change the autofocus options via the Active Information Display. The flash remains off, so if you'd like some fill-in flash (*see page 139*) you'll have to use a different mode (try ⚡, or one of the user-control modes). Alternatively, fit a separate flashgun. JPEG processing is based on a Standard Picture Control.

SPORTS MODE ☆
Sports mode is intended for rapid action: note how it freezes the spray as well as the rider.
200mm, 1/1000 sec., f/4, ISO 800.

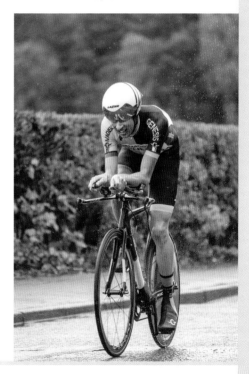

FUNCTIONS » SCENE MODES

THE EXPANDED GUIDE **41**

› 🌷 Close-up

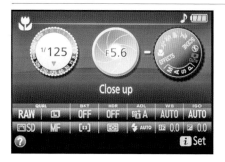

Close-up mode is of course intended for shooting at really close range. The camera sets a medium to small aperture to improve depth of field. This means shutter speeds can be low, so a tripod is often advisable to avoid camera shake. The built-in flash will activate automatically in low light, but it is a poor choice for close-up shots (*see page 161*): a separate accessory flashgun is a far better bet. You can also turn the flash off via the Active Information Display, or use 🍴 Food, when the flash does not activate automatically.

The camera automatically selects the central focus point, but this can be overridden very simply, using the Multi-selector. This is a good thing, as focus is particularly critical in close-up shooting and the key part of the subject will certainly not always be in the center of the frame. A Standard Picture Control is applied.

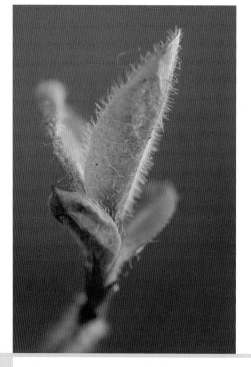

CLOSE-UP   «
A tripod is often essential in close-up shooting.
100mm macro, 1/50 sec., f/8, ISO 200, tripod.

› Night landscape

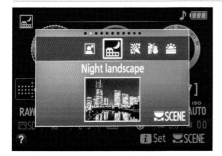

Night landscape mode allows long exposures to be used and therefore a tripod is strongly recommended. The built-in flash remains off but an accessory flash can be used. Images are processed to reduce noise and preserve colors, including the varied colors of artificial light. When exposures exceed 1 sec., Long Exposure noise reduction applies, which means there is a delay before another shot can be taken (*see page 43*). The maximum exposure time is 30 sec.; if a longer time is required, use Manual (M) mode and exposure to Bulb (*see page 62*). JPEG processing is based on a Standard Picture Control.

NIGHT LANDSCAPE ⨯
Night landscape mode allows long exposures.
28mm, 1/10 sec., f/4.5, ISO 3200.

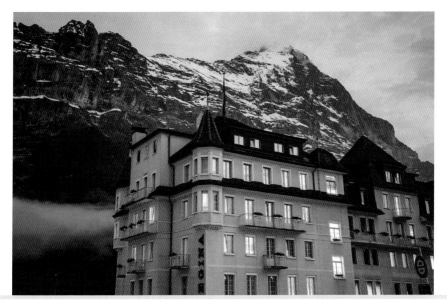

2 › 📷 Night portrait

› 🎉 Party/indoor

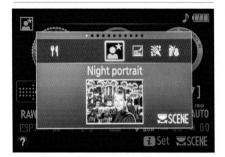

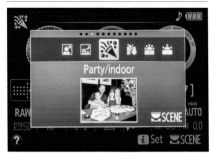

Night portrait mode is similar to Portrait mode, but when the ambient light is low it sets a long shutter speed to allow an image of the background to register. For this reason, a tripod or other solid camera support is recommended. The built-in flash operates automatically; results may be less harsh than regular Portrait mode but a flashgun improves results. JPEG processing is based on a Portrait Picture Control.

This mode is broadly similar to 📷 Night Portrait in seeking to record both people and their background, but does not allow such long exposures to be set. Again, Red-eye reduction flash is employed by default, complete with enforced shutter delay. Fortunately, Flash mode can be changed via the Active Information Display (*see page 30*). JPEG processing is based on a Standard Picture Control.

NIGHT PORTRAIT ⤜
Night portrait mode combines ambient lighting with on-board flash to capture the foreground and background. *28mm, 1/25 sec., f/5, ISO 800.*

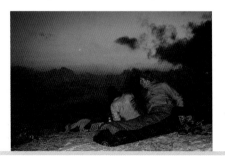

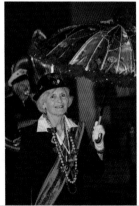

PARTY/ ⪡
INDOOR
Party/indoor mode can be used outdoors too. *66mm, 1/100 sec., f/4, ISO 3200.*

44   NIKON D5300

› ⛄ Beach/snow

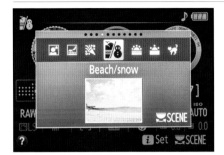

Beach and snow scenes are notorious for disappointing results—the subject is full of bright tones and yet pictures all too often turn out relatively dark. The D5300 aims to counteract this, partly by applying exposure compensation (*see page 66*) and partly through image processing. The built-in flash remains off, despite the fact that strong lighting conditions often suggest the use of fill-in flash (*see page 139*); however, you can use an accessory flashgun. JPEG processing is based on a Landscape Picture Control.

BEACH/SNOW ⌄
Beach/snow mode preserves a light, bright feel. *18mm, 1/500 sec., f/11, ISO 200.*

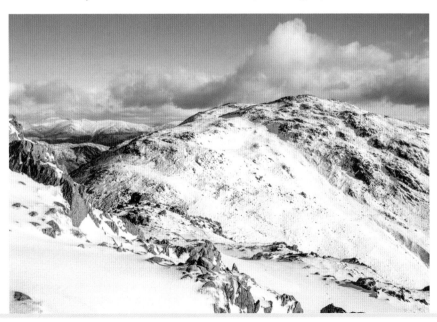

2

› ☀ Sunset

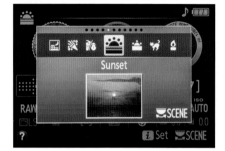

Sunset mode is similar in most respects to Night landscape. The built-in flash remains off, though an accessory flash can be used to light the foreground; long exposure times are possible and a tripod is recommended. Unlike Night landscape, however, white balance is predetermined, in order to preserve the vivid tones of the sky. JPEG processing is based on a Landscape Picture Control.

SUNSET ⪢
Sunset mode is biased towards vivid colors in the sky. *300mm, 1/60 sec., f/10, ISO 100.*

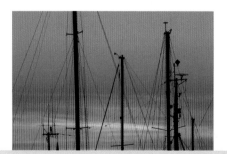

› ☀ Dusk/dawn

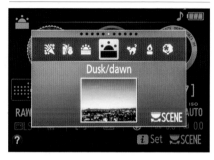

Dusk/dawn mode is also similar, but allows for the more muted colors and lower contrast usually experienced before sunrise and after sunset—again, white balance is predetermined rather than automatic. Flash remains off (though, as ever, an external flashgun can be used) and a tripod is recommended. JPEG processing is based on a Landscape Picture Control.

DUSK/DAWN ⪢
Dusk/dawn mode preserves the subtle hues and tones before sunrise and after sunset. *62mm, 1/160 sec., f/10, ISO 1600.*

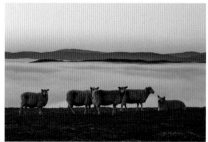

› 🐾 Pet portrait

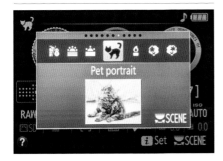

› 🕯 Candlelight

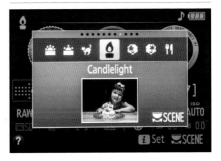

Recommended for portraits of active pets. The built-in flash will fire automatically in low light but the AF-assist illuminator turns off, presumably to avoid disturbing the animal before the shot. The flash can be turned off via the Active Information Display. In other respects this mode is very similar to 🎒 Child, including the use of a Standard Picture Control.

Recommended for portraits and other subjects illuminated by candlelight. Because candlelight is quite weak, exposure times are usually long, a tripod is recommended, and the subject will need to keep still. The built-in flash does not fire; it's possible to use an external flash but this generally defeats the object of shooting by candlelight. White balance is predetermined to allow for the very red hue of the candlelight. JPEG processing is based on a Standard Picture Control.

PET PORTRAIT ⩢
It's not exactly a pet, but Pet portrait mode still works well. *66mm, 1/1250 sec., f/4.5, ISO 400.*

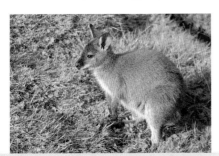

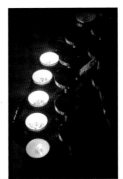

CANDLELIGHT ≪
Candlelight mode does not completely neutralize the warm glow of the candlelight. *70mm, 1/125 sec., f/4.5, ISO 3600.*

› ❀ Blossom

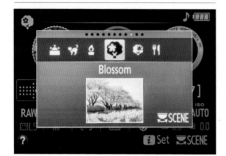

› ❀ Autumn colors

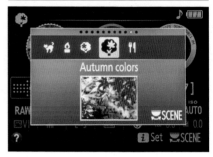

This mode is ideal for blossom, flowers, and similar subjects because colors are intense, the blooms reflect a lot of light, and detail is often lost. The camera employs Active D-Lighting (*see page 98*) to retain detail in highlight areas. JPEG processing (based on a Landscape Picture Control) aims to keep colors vivid but not garish. The built-in flash remains off and a tripod may be required in poor light.

This mode tackles similar issues, aiming to preserve the colors in autumn foliage, but processing favors the red and yellow parts of the spectrum. You could try it with other subjects where these colors are paramount. Again, the built-in flash remains off and a tripod may be needed. JPEG processing is based on a Vivid Picture Control.

BLOSSOM ❯❯

Blossom mode preserves delicate tone and detail in flowers and similar subjects. *200mm, 1/160 sec., f/7.1, ISO 100.*

AUTUMN COLORS ❯❯

Autumn colors mode favors vivid hues and emphasises red and yellow colors in the image. *40mm, 1/100 sec., f/7.1, ISO 100.*

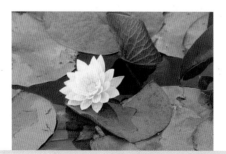

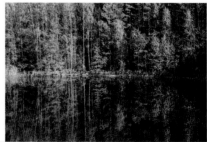

› ¶¶ Food

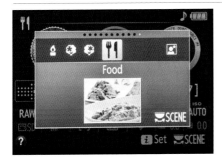

Recommended for detailed and vivid photos of food, this mode is unique among the D5300's Scene modes in that the built-in flash does not operate automatically but can be activated manually with the ⚡ button. However, because food photos are naturally taken at close range, the built-in flash often produces unwanted shadows (*see page 141*); if the lighting is too dim for a handheld shot, it is usually better to use a separate flash or to employ a tripod. This mode can be handy for shooting other close-up subjects without flash. JPEG processing is based on a Standard Picture Control.

> **Note:**
> A growing number of restaurants are now asking customers not to photograph their food, with or without flash. It's always a good idea to consider the possible annoyance to other diners.

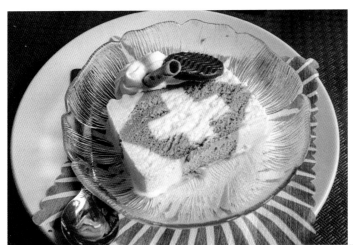

FOOD «
Food mode allows close-up shots without flash. *35mm, 1/100 sec., f/11, ISO 800.*

» SPECIAL EFFECTS MODES

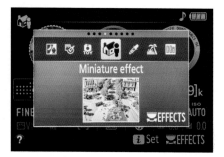

Special Effects modes are Scene modes taken to extremes, producing various striking effects through a combination of shooting settings and image processing. They always produce JPEG images: even if you have Image Quality set to RAW, the camera will create a JPEG image (Fine quality) instead. Some of these effects can also be applied to existing images through the Retouch menu.

In most of these modes, the built-in flash does not operate; a separate, accessory flash can be used but will often undermine the effect.

Effects modes can be used in Live View or Movie mode. This (usually) gives a preview of the effect, which is helpful. For some modes, like 🖋 Selective Color, Live View is essential. In 🎨 Color Sketch, 📷 Toy Camera Effect, and 🏠 Miniature Effect, shooting in Live View/movie allows you to adjust the strength of the effect (press 🆗 to see options).

To use Special Effects modes:

1) Set the Mode Dial to EFFECTS.

2) Rotate the Command Dial to select the required mode, referring to the Information Display (this is just like selecting Scene modes with the dial set to SCENE).

3) In Live View, press 🆗 to reveal shooting/ processing options, if the current mode offers any. Choose from the options and press 🆗 again to continue.

The following modes are available.

🎞 Night Vision

Uses extreme high ISO settings (maximum Hi 4 or ISO 102400); produces monochrome images. Autofocus is available only in Live View/movie shooting, and not always then: manual focus may be required. No options (except that exposure compensation is available); built-in flash is not available.

> **Tip**
>
> *Night Vision does allow handheld shooting in remarkably low light— but it's mono only, and quality is compromised. Using a tripod is usually a better bet.*

Color Sketch

Turns a photo into something resembling a colored pencil drawing. Movies can be recorded; the Nikon Reference Manual says they play back like a slide show or series of stills but I haven't found this to be true. The built-in flash is available. There are Live View options for Vividness and Outlines.

HDR Painting

This is rather like a combination of HDR (high dynamic range) (*see page 102*) and Color Sketch, producing an (allegedly) "painterly" effect. There are no options to control the effect and you can't preview it in Live View. The built-in flash is not available and you can't use HDR Painting when shooting movies (if the camera is set to this mode, movies will be shot in Auto (flash off) mode).

HDR PAINTING

You might find the HDR Painting effect an acquired taste or just what you need.

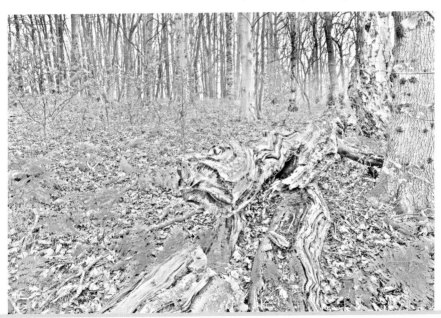

Toy Camera Effect

Mimics the effect of shooting with a plastic-lensed "toy" camera (or the result of the popular Instagram filters) by creating a color cast and strong vignetting. The built-in flash is available. There are Live View options for Vividness and Vignetting.

Miniature Effect

Mimics the recent fad for shooting images with extremely small and localized depth of field (*see page 60, 133*), making real landscapes or city views look like miniature models. The built-in flash is not available. When used for movie shooting, clips play back at high speed. Live View options: use the Multi-selector to position the in-focus zone.

Selective Color

Select particular color(s); other hues are rendered in monochrome. Colors can only be selected in Live View (select the color under the focus point by pressing ▲). This selection remains active if you then exit Live View and take shots using the Viewfinder, but the Viewfinder does not preview the effect (*see page 133*). The built-in flash is not available.

Silhouette

The camera's metering favors bright backgrounds such as vivid skies; foreground subjects record as silhouettes. This is most effective for subjects with interesting outlines. No options; built-in flash not available.

High key

Produces images filled with light tones, usually with no blacks or deep tones at all. It's not clear, in practical terms, whether this mode does anything more than generate simple overexposure. No options; built-in flash not available.

Low key

Low key is basically the opposite, creating a deep, low-toned image. Again, it's not clear whether this mode does anything more than simply underexpose the image. No options; built-in flash not available.

» USER-CONTROL MODES

The remaining four modes are traditional standards, which will be familiar to any experienced photographer. As well as allowing direct control over the basic settings of aperture and shutter speed (even in P mode through flexible program), these modes give full access to controls like White Balance (*page 80*), Active D-Lighting (*page 98*), and to Nikon Picture Controls (*page 99*). These extra controls give you great control over the look and feel of the image.

› (P) Programmed auto

In P mode the camera sets a combination of shutter speed and aperture that will give correctly exposed results in most situations. Of course, this much is also true of the Full Auto modes and Scene modes, but P mode allows you to adjust other parameters to suit your own creative ideas, including White Balance (*page 80*), Active

PROGRAMMED AUTO ⌄
This mode allows you to tailor camera settings to suit your own creative ideas. *200mm, 1/200 sec., f/5.6, ISO 400.*

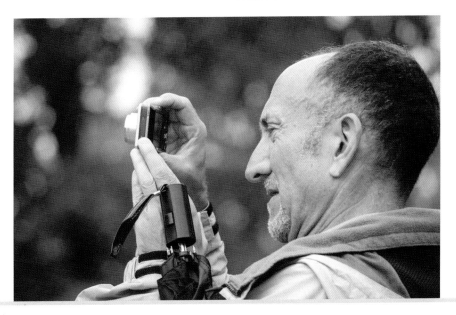

2

D-Lighting (*page 98*), and Nikon Picture Controls (*page 99*). It also allows manual selection of ISO rating (*page 85*).

You can change things even more in P mode through options like flexible program (see below), exposure lock (*page 67*), and exposure compensation (*page 66*), and you have complete freedom to use flash—or not—as you wish.

1) Rotate the Mode Dial to position **P**.

2) Frame the picture.

3) Half-depress the release button to activate focusing and exposure. The focus point(s) are displayed in the Viewfinder image and shutter speed and aperture settings appear at the bottom of the Viewfinder.

4) Fully depress the shutter release to take the picture.

Flexible program

Without leaving P mode you can change the combination of shutter speed and aperture by rotating the Command Dial. While flexible program is in effect the **P** indication in the Information Display changes to **P***. The shutter speed/aperture combination in the Viewfinder can be seen to change.

This does not change the overall exposure, i.e. it does not make the picture darker or lighter. What it does do is shift the combination of shutter speed and aperture. This gives you a speedy way to choose, for example, a faster shutter speed to freeze action, or a smaller aperture to increase depth of field (*page 60*), quickly gaining much of the control that S or A modes offer.

› (P) Shutter-priority auto

In Shutter-priority (S) mode, you control the shutter speed while the camera sets an appropriate aperture to give correctly exposed results in most situations. Control of shutter speed is key for moving subjects (*see page 56*). You can set speeds between 30 sec. and 1/4000 sec. Fine-tuning of exposure is possible through exposure lock (*page 67*), exposure compensation (*page 66*), and possibly auto bracketing (*page 68*).

1) Rotate the Mode Dial to position S.

2) Frame the picture.

3) Half-depress the release button to activate focusing and exposure. The focus point(s) will be displayed in the Viewfinder image and shutter speed and aperture settings appear at the bottom of the Viewfinder. Rotate the Command Dial to alter the shutter speed; the aperture will adjust automatically.

4) Fully depress the shutter release to take the picture.

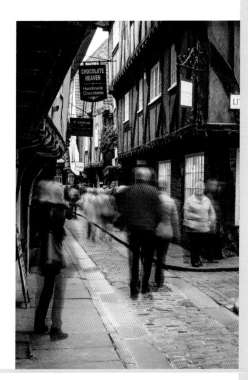

SHUTTER-PRIORITY »
A slow shutter speed blurred the people, but the buildings are sharp. The camera was steadied by a beanbag braced against a wall. (It wasn't practical to set up a tripod in the crowded confines of the Shambles in York.)
38mm, 2 sec., f/29, ISO 100.

Still photos can capture motion in many different ways and frequently reveal drama and grace that may be missed with the naked eye or in a movie. Here are two alternative approaches. Both are illustrated from cycling but could apply to most other kinds of action.

› Freezing the action

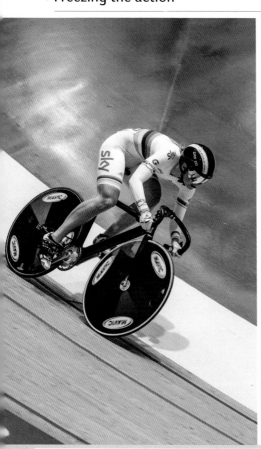

The D5300's Sports mode uses fast shutter speeds to freeze the action, while in Shutter-priority and Manual modes you can control the shutter speed directly. The D5300's fastest setting is 1/4000sec., but you'll rarely need this to capture a sharp image. The exact shutter speed needed depends not just on the raw speed of the subject, but on other factors like distance from the camera and direction of movement (e.g. across the frame or directly towards you). Often you'll have to experiment to see what works; warm-up laps before a race are useful for this, but remember that speeds will be higher in the race proper.

BLUR ON THE TRACK **«**
For this shot I used a shutter speed of 1/800 sec. This was as fast as I could get with an ISO of 3200—I don't like to use ISOs above this unless there's really no alternative. Even with the fast shutter speed I used a panning technique to keep the rider centered in the frame, and if you look closely you can see a little blur in the track, and even more in the wheels. *86mm, 1/800 sec., f/4, ISO 3200.*

› Panning

Panning captures movement very differently. By following the subject with the camera, it is recorded crisply (more or less) while the background becomes blurred. You can use relatively slow shutter speeds—anything from 1/8–1/125 sec. can be a good starting point, but you'll need to experiment. There's no way to do this in Sports mode, which means that Shutter-priority and Manual are really the only viable choices. Panning is usually easiest with a standard or short telephoto lens, provided you can get far enough back from the action.

IMPRESSION OF SPEED ≫
A panning shot with an extra dimension, using flash to give a sharp image of the rider; this combines with the blurred image from the panning motion to give a strong impression of speed. *40mm, 1/15 sec., f/10, ISO 320.*

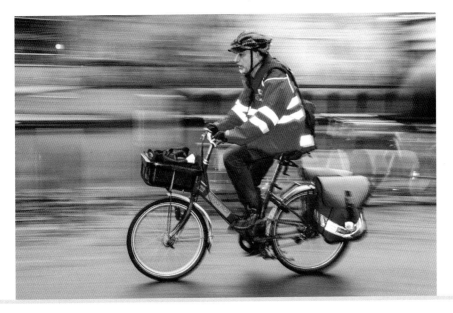

› (A) Aperture-priority auto

In Aperture-priority (A) mode, you control the aperture while the camera sets an appropriate shutter speed to give correctly exposed results in most situations. Control of aperture is particularly useful for regulating depth of field (*see page 60*).

The range of apertures available is limited by the lens that's fitted, not by the camera.

Fine-tuning of exposure is possible through exposure lock (*page 67*), exposure compensation (*page 66*), and possibly auto bracketing (*page 68*).

1) Rotate the Mode Dial to position **A**.

2) Frame the picture.

3) Half-depress the release button to activate focusing and exposure. The focus point(s) will be displayed in the Viewfinder, and shutter speed and aperture settings will appear below the Viewfinder image.

4) Rotate the Command Dial to alter the aperture; the shutter speed will adjust automatically. The Information Display (in Graphic mode) also shows a graphic representation of the aperture.

5) Fully depress the shutter release to take the picture.

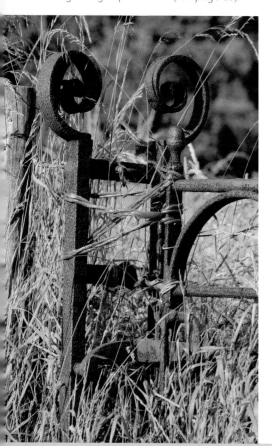

APERTURE CONTROL **«**
The combination of lens, shooting distance, and aperture mean the background is suitably soft and doesn't clutter or confuse the image.
200mm, 1/200 sec., f/10, ISO 250.

Depth of field preview

When you look through the D5300's Viewfinder, the lens is set at its widest aperture; if a smaller aperture is selected, the lens stops down at the moment the picture is actually taken. As a result, the Viewfinder image may have much less depth of field than the final shot. Many Nikon DSLRs, but not the D5300, have a depth of field preview button—this stops the lens down to the selected aperture. However, it also darkens the image and assessing sharpness isn't always easy.

In any case, there are other options. One is by using Live View. When you enter Live View, the camera stops down to the currently set aperture. However, it doesn't immediately readjust if you change the aperture setting with the Command Dial. It will only reset the aperture when you take a picture, or exit and resume Live View.

You can also get a sense of depth of field by taking a test shot and then reviewing it on the monitor. Both Live View and image review allow you to zoom in.

SNOWMAN　　　　　　　　　　　　⌄
Focus was on the snowman but a good depth of field means the background is still clear. *28mm, 1/160 sec., f/11, ISO 200.*

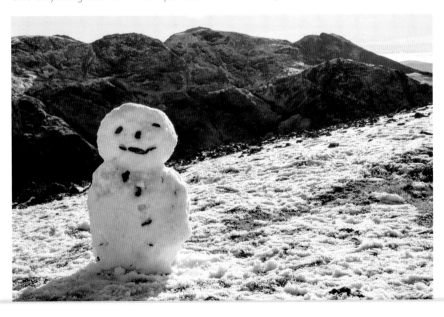

Depth of field describes the zone in front of and behind the actual point of focus in which objects appear to be sharp in the final image.

Aperture is only one of the factors influencing depth of field. The other key factors are the focal length of the lens and the distance to the subject. With long lenses and/or nearby subjects, depth of field may remain quite shallow even at small apertures.

Sometimes a shallow depth of field is exactly what you want, as it makes the subject stand out against a soft background. This is common with portraits, for example, and is also often seen in sports and wildlife photography—though in these genres the frequent combination of a long lens and fast shutter speed means that shallow depth of field is more of a necessity than a completely free choice.

SHALLOW DEPTH OF FIELD ⌄
Using a long lens at its widest aperture on a fairly close subject, depth of field is undeniably shallow: the eye is sharp but even the feathers on the breast are a little soft. *300mm, 1/400 sec., f/4, ISO 400.*

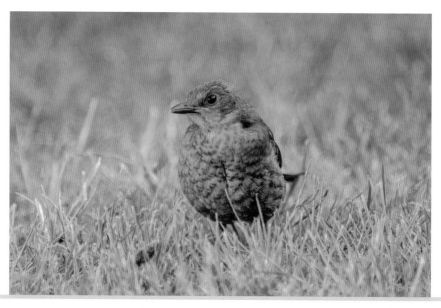

For other images you may want to try and have everything sharp from front to back: this is the traditional approach in landscape photography, for instance. When you're shooting landscapes, which have no single "subject", where you place the focus point in a scene can be quite important. You can use "hyperfocal distance" calculators or a rule of thumb such as "the far end of the foreground".

If you really want to maximize depth of field, you need to try and stack all three key factors (focal length, aperture, and distance) in your favor. This isn't always possible and you may have to decide which area is more important—foreground or background.

CLASSIC LANDSCAPE ⌄
This is a demonstration of the classic landscape photographer's approach: wide-angle lens, small aperture, and focus point in the middle ground.
15mm, 1/40 sec., f/11, ISO 320.

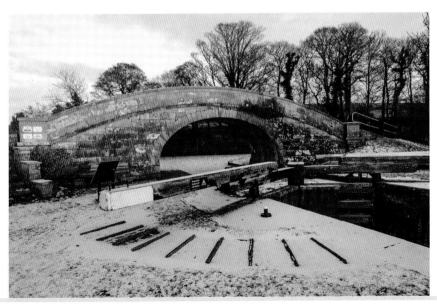

2 › (M) Manual Mode

In M mode, you control both shutter speed and aperture for maximum creative flexibility. Manual mode is most comfortably employed when shooting without pressure of time or in fairly constant light conditions, but many experienced photographers use it all the time to retain complete control.

Shutter speeds can be set between 30 sec. and 1/4000 sec., plus B or "bulb" (in which the shutter remains open indefinitely while the shutter release is depressed). The range of apertures that can be set is limited by the lens that's fitted to the camera.

1) Press the Mode Dial release and rotate the dial to position **M**.

2) Frame the picture.

3) Half-press the release button to activate focusing and exposure metering. The focus point(s) will be displayed in the Viewfinder

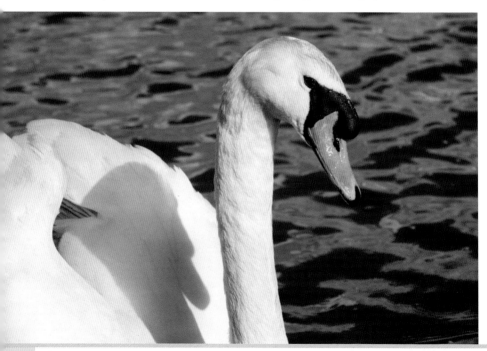

and shutter speed and aperture settings will appear below the Viewfinder image. Check the analog exposure display in the Viewfinder (and/or the playback histogram), and if necessary adjust settings to achieve correct exposure.

4) Rotate the Command Dial to alter the shutter speed.

5) Hold ⊞ and rotate the Command Dial to alter the aperture.

6) Fully depress the shutter release to take the picture.

> ### *Tip*
>
> *B ("bulb"), with its unlimited exposure duration, is only available in M mode. As such it's the only possible choice for exposures longer than 30 sec., which you're likely to need for starry skies, fireworks displays, and so on.*

Using the Analog exposure displays

In Manual Mode, an analog exposure display appears in the center of the Viewfinder readouts and in the Information Display. This shows whether the photograph would be under- or overexposed at current settings. Adjust shutter speed and/or aperture until the indicator is aligned with the **0** mark in the center of the display: the exposure now matches the camera's recommendations. The D5300's metering is good enough that this will generally be correct, but if time allows it is often helpful to review the image and check the histogram display (see Playback, *page 96*) after taking a shot. If necessary, you can then make adjustments for creative effect or to achieve a specific result. The Analog exposure display also appears in P, S, and A modes when you apply Exposure compensation (*see page 66*).

MANUAL MODE   **«**
This subject was challenging in terms of exposure; it was important to retain detail both in the white feathers and in the black skin at the base of the swan's bill. I used manual mode and checked the histogram after the first shot.
105mm, 1/1000 sec., f/10, ISO 320.

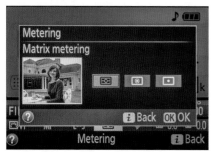

SELECTING METERING MODE IN THE ACTIVE INFORMATION DISPLAY ☆

To ensure that images are correctly exposed, the camera must measure the light levels; this is known as exposure metering. The D5300 provides three different metering modes, which should cover any eventuality. Switch between them using the Metering item in the Active Information Display (this is only possible in the User-control modes—in other modes, matrix metering is automatically selected).

› 3D Color Matrix Metering II

Using a 2016-pixel color sensor, 3D Color Matrix Metering II analyzes data on the brightness, color, and contrast of the scene. When a Type G or D Nikkor lens is fitted, the system also analyzes distance information based on where the camera focuses—that's why it's called 3D. With other CPU lenses, this distance information is not used and metering automatically reverts to a non-3D version.

Matrix metering is recommended for the vast majority of shooting and will nearly always produce excellent results.

› Center-weighted metering

This is a very traditional form of metering. The camera meters from the entire frame, but gives greater weight (75%) to a central circle—on the D5300 it's 8mm across. Center-weighted metering is useful in areas like portraiture, where the key subject often occupies the central portion of the frame (although ♞ Portrait mode sticks with matrix metering).

› Spot metering

☒ In this mode the camera meters solely from a small (3.5mm) circular area. This circle is centered on the current focus point, allowing you to meter from an off-center subject. (This does not apply if Auto-area AF (AF-A) is in use, when the metering point is the center of the frame.)

Spot metering can be very useful when an important subject is very much darker or lighter than the background and you want to be sure it is correctly exposed

(matrix metering is more likely to compromise between subject and background).

SPOT ON ☒

With brilliantly-lit clouds above, and deep shadows below, contrast was very high. Shooting in RAW, the camera was able to capture detail in both the highlights and shadows, but only if the exposure was exactly right. Spot metering helped me strike that balance. *50mm, 1/500 sec., f/11, ISO 200.*

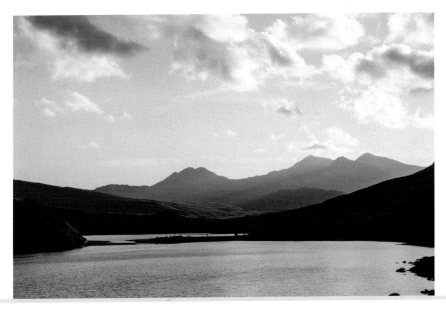

The D5300 will deliver accurate exposures under most conditions, but no camera is infallible. Nor can it read your mind or anticipate your creative ideas. Sometimes it needs a little help to get the result spot-on.

All metering systems still work partly on the assumption that key subject areas have a middling tonal value (like the "gray cards" inside the covers of this book), and should appear as a mid-tone in the images. With subjects which are very pale or very dark, this can give inaccurate results. We've all seen pictures where brilliant white snow has turned out gray: normal metering has tried to reproduce it as mid-tones, making it darker than it should be. Where very dark tones predominate, the converse is true. To get these tones right, you may have to tell the camera to make the exposure a little lighter or darker; this is exposure compensation.

The principle is simple: to make the subject lighter (to keep light tones looking light), increase exposure by using positive compensation. Conversely, to keep dark tones looking dark, use negative compensation. Digital cameras take the guesswork out of this process, because you can check after shooting and have another go if necessary. The highlights display (*page 97*), and especially the histogram (*page 96*) are extremely helpful for this.

If this judgement is difficult, or lighting conditions are particularly extreme, an extra level of "insurance" is available through exposure bracketing (*see page 68*).

Exposure compensation is only available in P, S, and A modes, plus 🌙 Night Vision. In M mode ±️ controls the aperture, but you can "compensate" simply by setting shutter speed and/or aperture so that the meter readout shows a + or − value. In Auto, Scene, and Effects modes (other than 🌙), exposure control is fully automatic, although you can still use Exposure lock (see next page).

› **Using exposure compensation**

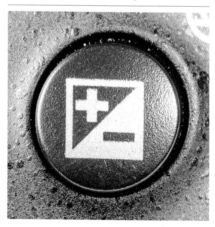

EXPOSURE COMPENSATION BUTTON ⌃

1) Exposure compensation can be applied in steps of $^1/_3$ Ev (default) or $^1/_2$ Ev, depending on the option selected for Custom setting b1. (This also dictates the steps used for general exposure control, e.g. aperture steps in A or M mode.)

2) Press ⊞ and rotate the Command Dial to set negative or positive compensation; the chosen value is shown in the Information Display and in the Viewfinder. Compensation can be set between −5 Ev and +5 Ev, though you'll rarely need these extremes.

3) Release ⊞. ⊞ appears in the Viewfinder, and the Analog Exposure Display appears with a blinking **0** at its center.

4) Take the picture as normal. If time allows, check that the result is satisfactory.

Tip

Reset exposure compensation (step 5) as soon as possible; otherwise it will apply to later shots which don't need it. It is not reset automatically even when the camera is switched off.

5) To restore normal exposure settings, press ⊞ and rotate the Command Dial until the value returns to **0.0**.

› Exposure lock

Exposure lock is another way to fine-tune the camera's exposure setting; many people find this a quick and intuitive method. It's useful, for instance, in situations where very dark or light areas (especially light sources) within the frame can over-influence exposure. Exposure lock helps you to meter from a more average area, by allowing you to point the camera in a different direction or step closer to the subject, and then hold that exposure while re-framing the shot you want. Unlike exposure compensation, it can be used in Scene modes.

Note:
Nikon advises against using exposure lock when you're using matrix metering, but there's absolutely no reason not to do so if it helps you get the desired result.

Using Exposure lock

1) Aim the camera in a different direction, or zoom the lens to avoid the potentially problematic dark or light areas. If you're using center-weighted or spot metering, look for areas of middling tone (but which are receiving the same sort of light as the main subject).

2) Half-press the shutter to take a meter reading, then keep it pressed as you press *AE-L/AF-L* to lock the exposure value.

3) Keep *AE-L/AF-L* half-pressed as you reframe the image, then press down fully to shoot.

By default, *AE-L/AF-L* locks focus as well as exposure. This can be changed using Custom setting f2 (*see page 119*).

› Exposure bracketing

Another way to ensure that you capture a correctly exposed image is to take several frames at differing exposures, and then select the best one; this is called exposure bracketing. The D5300 allows you to bracket three exposures automatically, with up to 2 Ev between each. Bracketing is only available in P, S, A, and M modes.

1) Ensure that Custom setting e2 is set to **AE bracketing** (this is the default setting).

2) In the Active Information Display, highlight **BKT** and press (OK), then use the Multi-selector to select the exposure differential between shots in the sequence (from 0.3 Ev to 2 Ev, shown as AE0.3 to AE2.0).

3) Press (OK) again. **AE-BKT** is shown in the Information Display and **BKT** in the Viewfinder.

4) Frame, focus, and shoot normally. The camera will vary the exposure with each frame. Continuous release mode (*see page 32*) is useful for this; the camera will pause at the end of the three shots.

5) To cancel, repeat step 2 and select **OFF**.

If the memory card becomes full before the sequence is complete, the camera will stop shooting. Replace the card, or delete images to make space; the camera will then resume where it left off. If you turn the camera off in mid-sequence, when you next you switch it on it will resume the sequence from where it left off.

> ### *Tip*
>
> *The D5300 offers other forms of bracketing: choose between them using Custom setting e2 (*see page 119*). Instead of AE bracketing (as described here), you can bracket White Balance or Active D-Lighting.*

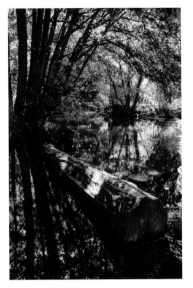

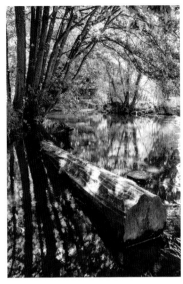

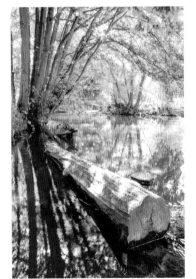

EXPOSURE BRACKETING

The lighting was very tricky here and exposure bracketing let me hedge my bets: −1 Ev (top left); 0 Ev (above); +1 Ev (left). *18mm, $^1/_4$, $^1/_8$, $^1/_{15}$ sec., f/11, ISO 200, tripod.*

Tip

Exposure bracketing isn't ideal when shooting moving subjects, as the best exposure rarely coincides with the subject being in the best position. If possible, use other means to get the exposure right beforehand.

In the end, getting the exposure "right" isn't about matching some technical definition of what's correct; it's about making sure that images look the way you want them to look. However, you will generally want to preserve detail in both shadows and highlights as far as possible.

Most of the time, the camera does a very good job of determining exposure, and will almost always get results that are close enough that you can make the final adjustments in post-processing (especially if you shoot RAW).

However, the times when it may fall short are precisely the times when it matters most: when you want to make a really strong statement with an image, or when the light and the elements are at their most striking. This is when it really

DYNAMIC LIGHT
This is not so much a landscape as a skyscape—yet try covering up the bottom of the image and it's clear that the land still adds depth, context, and a sense of scale. However, exposure was very much based on getting the sky right—I was keen to retain highlight detail but less concerned if the trees were effectively black. *18mm, 1/250 sec., f/11, ISO 100.*

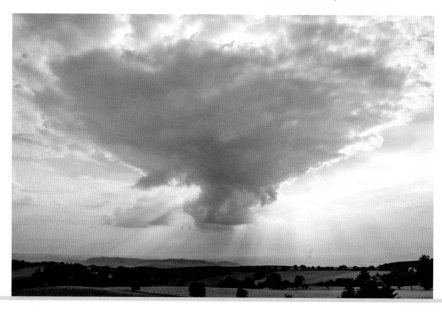

pays to make the small extra effort of checking exposure carefully and making an adjustment if necessary, perhaps either by using exposure compensation or by shooting in Manual mode.

Soft light presents different challenges. Exposure determination is usually easy and the camera rarely gets it far wrong; the issue, instead, is that soft light, with its lack of strong shadows and contrast, can easily lead to images that look flat or dull. It can work well, however, for subjects with strong colors, shapes, or patterns.

SOFT LIGHT   »
Some people might have seen this as a dull day, but I found it visually very stimulating. There's a subtle but rich palette of color and there is also a strong sense of perspective with several "markers" at different distances, such as the nearby trees, the distant plantation, and the profile of the ridge, as well as the mist. *20mm, 1/80 sec., f/11, ISO 200, tripod.*

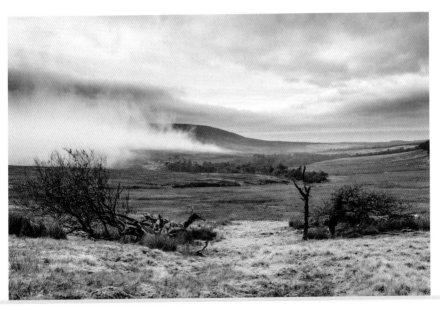

2 » FOCUSING

Focusing is not simply about ensuring that "the picture" is in focus. It's actually quite difficult, and sometimes impossible, to ensure that everything in an image appears sharp. The first essential is making sure that the camera focuses on the desired subject, or even—especially in close-up photography—the right part of the subject. Control of depth of field (*page 60*) then helps you determine how much of the rest of the image will also be sharp.

The various focus options boil down to how the camera focuses, determined by the focus modes, and where it focuses (what the subject is, if you like), determined by the AF-area modes.

› Focus modes

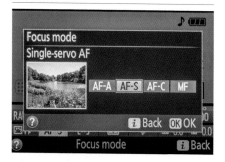

FOCUS MODE SELECTION

In the Active Information Display, select the Focus mode item (by default this reads **AF-A**). Press (OK) and select from the

available options; press (OK) again to confirm the selection and return to Shooting mode.

When the camera is in an Auto, Scene, or Effects mode, only two options are offered. Manual focus can always be selected, but the only autofocus option is AF-A. In P, S, A, or M mode four options are available.

> **Note:**
> This section deals only with focusing in normal shooting (i.e. using the Viewfinder). Focusing works differently in Live View (*page 90*) and movie shooting (*page 171*).

AF-A Auto-servo AF

By default the camera is set to AF-A in all exposure modes. AF-A means that the camera automatically switches between two autofocus modes: single-servo AF and continuous-servo AF (see below).

AF-S Single-servo AF

The camera focuses when the shutter release is pressed halfway. If you keep it half-pressed, focus remains locked on this point. The shutter cannot release to take a picture unless focus has been acquired (focus priority). This mode is recommended for accurate focusing on static subjects.

AF-C Continuous-servo AF

In this mode, recommended for moving subjects, the camera continues to seek focus as long as the shutter release is depressed: if the subject moves, the camera will refocus. The camera is able to take a picture even if it hasn't acquired perfect focus (release priority).

The D5300 employs predictive focus

CONTINUOUS AUTOFOCUS ☒

AF-C is recommended for moving subjects.
50mm, 1/800 sec., f/4, ISO 3200.

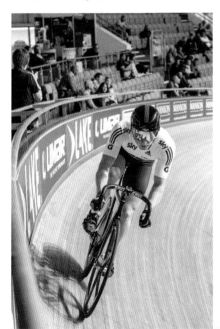

tracking: if the subject moves while continuous servo AF is active, the camera analyzes the movement and attempts to predict where the subject will be when the shutter is released.

› (M) Manual focus

When a camera has sophisticated AF capabilities, manual focus might appear redundant, but many photographers still value the extra control and involvement it offers. There are also certain subjects and circumstances that can bamboozle even the best AF systems. Manual focusing is a straightforward process, which hardly requires description: set the focus mode to MF and use the focusing ring on the lens to bring the subject into focus.

MANUAL FOCUS ☒

Key points in this image didn't coincide exactly with any of the AF points so I focused manually.
100mm macro, 1/200 sec., f/11, ISO 200, tripod.

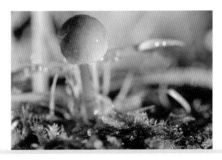

Focus confirmation

When using a lens that does not focus automatically with the D5300, you can still take advantage of the camera's focusing technology thanks to focus confirmation. It requires you to select an appropriate focus point, as if you were using autofocus. When the subject at that point is in focus, a green dot appears at far left of the Viewfinder data display. In P, S, and A modes you can also use the exposure display as a focus guide or rangefinder: enable this using Custom setting a4 Rangefinder (*page 116*).

› AF-area modes

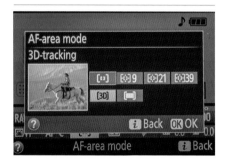

The D5300 has 39 focus points covering much of the frame (this area is indicated by a faint outline in the Viewfinder). To focus on the desired subject, it's vital that the camera uses appropriate focus point(s); this is the function of AF-area mode. Select AF-area mode in the Active Information Display.

By default, the camera selects the focus point automatically (Auto-area), but you can always change to manual selection in any shooting mode. However, the camera only "remembers" this selection in P, S, A, or M modes. If you change the default setting in any of the Auto or Scene modes it will remain in effect only as long as you remain in that exposure mode. For instance, if you switch from Portrait to Landscape and then back again, you'll find that the camera has reverted to Auto-area.

Auto-area [■]

In Auto-area, the D5300 selects the focus point automatically, effectively deciding what the subject is. When Type G or D lenses are used, Face Recognition allows the camera to distinguish a human subject from the background. Determining what the subject is seems a pretty basic decision—and the other AF-area modes let you do just that.

Single-point [ᴄɪ]

In this mode, you select the focus area, using the Multi-selector to move quickly through the 39 focus points. The chosen focus point is outlined in the Viewfinder. This mode is best suited to relatively static subjects, and marries naturally with AF-S autofocus mode.

Dynamic-area AF [⊡]

This mode is more complicated, as it has

several sub-modes. These can only be selected when the AF mode is AF-A or AF-C (*page 72*).

In all sub-modes, you still select the initial focus point, as in Single-area AF. If the subject moves, the camera will then employ other focus points to maintain focus, but it's still trying to track the subject you selected. The sub-mode options determine the number of focus points that will be employed for this: 9, 21, or the full 39 points.

The final option is 3D tracking, which uses a wide range of information, including subject colors, to track subjects that may be moving erratically.

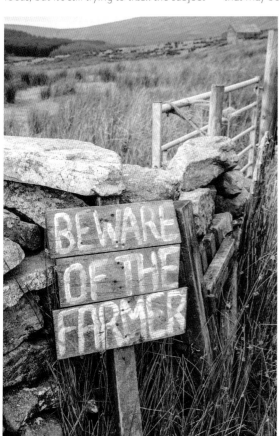

OFF-CENTER   **«**
The ability to select focus points is most helpful with off-center subjects, or if you want to focus on a very specific point. The sign is key and I chose to let the background go slightly soft.
30mm, 1/100 sec., f/5.6, ISO 200

Focus point selection

1) Ensure the camera is set to an AF-area mode other than 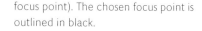 Auto-area.

2) Half-depress the shutter release to activate autofocus.

3) Using the Multi-selector, move the focus point to the desired position (pressing OK jumps directly to the central focus point). The chosen focus point is outlined in black.

4) Press the shutter-release button halfway to focus at the selected point; depress it fully to take the shot. If the AF-area mode is Dynamic-area AF, the focus point may move to track the subject.

› Focus lock

Though the 39 focus points cover a wide area, they do not extend to the edges of the frame. If you need to focus on a subject beyond the area they cover, the simplest procedure is as follows:

1) Adjust framing to bring the subject within the available focus area.

2) Select a focus point and focus on the subject in the normal way.

3) Lock focus. In AF-S mode, this can be done by keeping half-pressure on the shutter-release button, or by pressing and holding *AE-L/AF-L*. In AF-C mode, only *AE-L/AF-L* can be used.

4) Reframe the image as desired and press the shutter-release button fully to take the

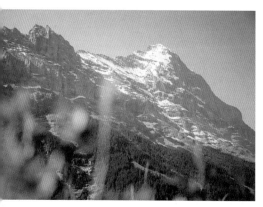

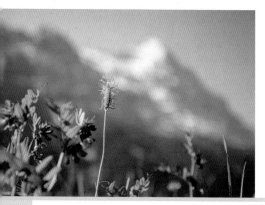

FOCUS SHIFT »
A fairly dramatic example of the effect of shifting the focus point. *35mm, 1/2000 sec., f/2.8, ISO 200.*

picture. If you maintain half-pressure on the shutter-release button (in AF-S), or hold *AE-L/AF-L* (in any AF mode), focus remains locked for further shots.

Focus lock really only works for static subjects. To maintain focus on moving subjects, make sure they are within the area covered by the focus points when you shoot.

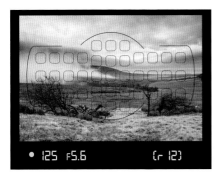

D5300 VIEWFINDER   ⌃
The Viewfinder displays the available focus areas as well as an in-focus indicator at the left of the menu bar.

> **Note:**
> At default settings, *AE-L/AF-L* locks exposure as well as focus, but this can be changed using Custom setting f4.

› AF-assist illuminator

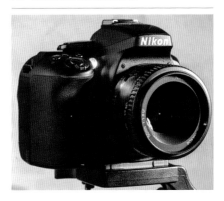

A small lamp is available to help the camera focus in dim light. It requires the camera to be in AF-S, and either the central focus point must be selected or AF-A must be engaged. If these conditions are met, it illuminates automatically when required. Obviously, its range is limited. It can be turned off using Custom setting a3, and is always off in some Scene modes.

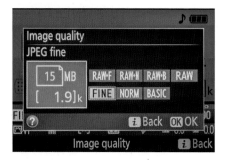

SETTING IMAGE QUALITY IN THE ACTIVE INFORMATION DISPLAY

The Image quality settings are not some miraculous shortcut to great pictures; that is still—thank goodness—the photographer's responsibility. Instead, "Image quality" refers to the file format, or the way that image data is recorded.

The D5300 offers a choice of two file types: NEF (RAW) and JPEG. The essential difference is that JPEG files are processed in-camera to produce files that should be usable right away (for instance, for direct printing from the memory card), without further processing on computer.

NEF (RAW) files, on the other hand, record image data from the sensor complete and unadulterated, without onboard processing. The generic term for such files is RAW or Camera RAW; NEF is a Nikon-specific variety of RAW file. Shooting RAW leaves much greater scope for processing later to achieve exactly the pictorial result you desire. RAW files can be recorded at either **12-bit** or **14-bit** depth. The 14-bit files capture four times more color information, but produce larger file sizes and the camera takes longer to transfer them to the memory card. As a result, the maximum continuous shooting rate drops from 5fps to 4fps. Even so, you can't shoot a long burst before the rate drops further.

The D5300 also allows you to capture two versions of the same image simultaneously, one NEF (RAW) and one JPEG. The JPEG serves for immediate needs while the RAW version can be processed later for the ultimate result.

It's often assumed that RAW is the "real" photographer's choice and JPEG is for the casual snapper, but it's not quite that clear-cut. You can get great results shooting JPEG (especially at Fine quality setting). However, there's less room to "fix" images later so, if you're serious about great results, shooting JPEG demands at least equal, if not greater care, especially in relation to exposure and white balance.

Some of the D5300's shooting modes do not allow you to capture RAW files, because image processing is integral to these modes. This applies to Effects modes (*see pages 50–52*) and also to HDR (high dynamic range) (*see page 102*). When you use the Retouch menu (*page 126*), the end product is a JPEG image.

Setting image quality

1) In the Active Information Display, **select Image quality**.

2) Press (OK) to bring up the list of options (see the table below). Using the Multi-selector, highlight the required setting then press (OK) again to make it effective.

Tip

If you've taken a shot in RAW but then wish you had a JPEG version, perhaps for immediate printing or to upload through WiFi, you can create one using the **NEF (RAW) Processing** *item in the Retouch Menu (*see page 126*).*

Image quality options

RAW	14-bit NEF (RAW) files are recorded for the ultimate quality and creative flexibility.
FINE	8-bit JPEG files are recorded with a compression ratio of approximately 1:4; should be suitable for prints of A3 size or even larger.
NORM	8-bit JPEG files are recorded with a compression ratio of approximately 1:8; should be suitable for modest-sized prints.
BASIC	8-bit JPEG files are recorded with a compression ratio of approximately 1:16, suitable for transmission by email or website use but not recommended for printing.
RAW + F **RAW + N** **RAW + B**	Two copies of the same image are recorded simultaneously, one NEF (RAW) and one JPEG (Fine, Normal, or Basic).

» WHITE BALANCE

For JPEG files, the D5300 offers three options for image size. **Large** is the maximum available size from the D5300's sensor, i.e. 6000 x 4000 pixels. **Medium** is 4496 x 3000 pixels, roughly equivalent to a 13.5-megapixel camera. **Small** is 2992 x 2000 pixels, roughly equivalent to a 6-megapixel camera. Even **Small** size images exceed the maximum resolution of an HD TV, or almost any computer monitor, and can yield reasonable prints up to at least 12 x 8 inches. **Medium** exceeds the resolution of the new breed of 4K TV sets.

RAW files are always recorded at the maximum size.

Setting image size

1) In the Active Information Display, select **Image size**. (If **Image quality** is set to **RAW** you will not be able to select this item.)

2) Press ⓞⓚ to show the list of options. Using the Multi-selector, highlight the required setting then press ⓞⓚ again to make it effective.

Light sources, natural and artificial, vary enormously in color. The human eye and brain are very good (though not perfect) at compensating for this and seeing people and objects in their "true" colors, so that we nearly always see grass as green, and so on. Digital cameras also have a capacity to compensate for the varying colors of light and, used correctly, the D5300 can produce natural-looking colors under almost any conditions you'll ever encounter.

The D5300 has a sophisticated system for determining white balance (WB) automatically, which produces good results most of the time. For finer control, or for creative effect, the D5300 also offers a range of user-controlled settings, but these are only accessible when using P, S, A, or M modes.

Tip

When shooting RAW images, the in-camera white balance setting is not crucial, as it can be adjusted in later processing. However, it affects how images look on playback and review, so there is still some value in setting WB appropriately.

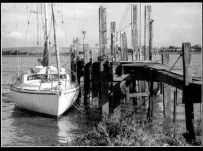

INCANDESCENT

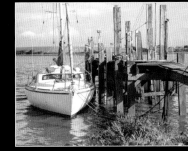

COOL-WHITE FLUORESCENT

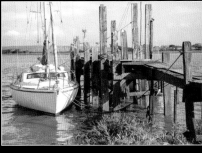

DIRECT SUNLIGHT

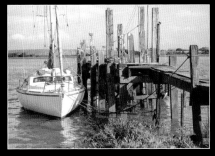

FLASH

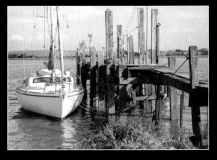

CLOUDY

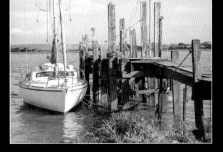

SHADE

Setting white balance

There are two ways to set white balance (three if you count the Fn button, *see page 119*).

Using the Active Information Display

1) In the Active Information Display, select the **WB** item and press (OK) to reveal a list of options.

2) Use the Multi-selector to highlight the required setting, then press (OK) to accept it.

Using the Shooting menu

This is a slower method but makes extra options available.

1) Press **MENU**, select **Shooting menu** and navigate to **White Balance**.

2) Press (OK) to reveal a list of options.

3) Use the Multi-selector to highlight the required setting, then press (OK). Alternatively press ▶.

4) If you press ▶, a graphical display appears. Using this, you can fine-tune the setting using the Multi-selector, or just press (OK) to accept the standard value.

5) If you select **Fluorescent** at step 3, a sub-menu appears from which you can select an appropriate type of fluorescent

lamp (see the table on the next page). You can then fine-tune this setting even further by pressing press ▶ as in step 4.

> **Note:**
> If you use the Active Information Display to select **Fluorescent**, the precise value will be whatever was last selected in the sub-menu under the Shooting menu. (The default is **4: Cool-white fluorescent**.)

› Preset Manual White Balance

You can set the white balance to precisely match any lighting conditions by taking a reference photo of a neutral object. Frankly, this is a cumbersome procedure that few will ever employ (see the *Nikon Reference Manual* for details—it takes two pages). It's normally much easier to shoot RAW and tweak the white balance later; a reference photo can also be helpful for this when high precision is required.

> **Note:**
> The endpapers of this book are designed to serve as "gray cards", ideal for reference photos for these purposes.

Icon	Menu option	Color temperature (°K)	Description
AUTO	Auto	3500–8000	Camera sets WB automatically, based on information from imaging and metering sensors. Most accurate with Type G and Type D lenses.
☀	Incandescent	3000	Use under incandescent (tungsten) lighting, e.g. traditional household bulbs.
	Fluorescent (Submenu offers seven options):		
	1) Sodium-vapor lamps	2700	Use under sodium-vapor lighting, often used in sports venues.
	2) Warm-white fluorescent	3000	Use in warm-white fluorescent lighting.
	3) White fluorescent	3700	Use in white fluorescent lighting.
☀	**4)** Cool-white fluorescent	4200	Use in cool-white fluorescent lighting.
	5) Day white fluorescent	5000	Use in daylight white fluorescent lighting.
	6) Daylight fluorescent	6500	Use in daylight fluorescent lighting.
	7) High temp. mercury-vapor	7200	Use in high color temperature lighting, e.g. mercury vapor lamps.
☀	Direct sunlight	5200	Use for subjects in direct sunlight.
⚡	Flash	5400	Use with built-in flash or separate flashgun.
☁	Cloudy	6000	Use in daylight, under cloudy/overcast skies.
⌂	Shade	8000	Use on sunny days for subjects in shade.
K	Choose color temp.	2500–10,000	Select color temperature from list of values.
PRE	Preset Manual	n/a	Derive white balance direct from subject or lightsource, or from an existing photo.

2

Note:
Energy-saving bulbs, which have largely replaced traditional incandescent (tungsten) bulbs, are compact fluorescent units. Their color temperature varies but many of those in domestic use are rated around 2700°K, equivalent to Fluorescent setting **1 Sodium-vapor lamps**. In case of doubt, it's always a good idea to take test shots if possible, or allow for later adjustment by shooting RAW files.

Tip

If images consistently appear color-shifted on your computer screen, compensating by adjusting the camera's white balance is probably not the answer; the problem may well be with the computer screen settings (see page 222).

> ## Color space

Color spaces define the range (or gamut) of colors which can be recorded. Like most DSLRs, the Nikon D5300 offers a choice between sRGB and Adobe RGB color spaces. The chosen color space will apply to all shots taken in all exposure modes. To select the color space, use the **Color space** item in the Shooting menu.

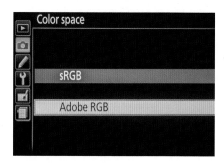

SETTING COLOR SPACE IN THE SHOOTING MENU

sRGB (the default setting) has a narrower gamut but images often appear brighter and more punchy. It's the standard color space on the Internet and in photo printing stores, for example, and is a safe choice for images that are likely to be used or printed straight off, with little or no post-processing.

Adobe RGB has a wider gamut and is commonly used in professional printing and reproduction. It's a better choice for images that are destined for professional applications or where significant post-processing is anticipated. However, images straight from the camera may look slightly dull on most computers and web devices or if printed without full color management.

» ISO SENSITIVITY SETTINGS

The ISO setting governs the camera's sensitivity to greater or lesser amounts of light. At higher ISO settings, less light is needed to capture an acceptable image. As well as accommodating lower light levels, higher ISOs are also useful when you need a small aperture for increased depth of field (*see page 60*) or a fast shutter speed to freeze rapid movement (*see page 56*).

Conversely, lower ISOs are useful in brighter conditions, and/or when you want to use wide apertures or slow shutter speeds. The D5300 offers ISO settings from 100 to 12,800. Image noise (*see page 113*) does increase at higher settings. The D5300 manages this well, but you may still find noise levels at the highest ISOs exceed your tolerance—try a few shots and see for yourself.

There are additional Hi settings beyond the standard range. These are Hi0.3 (equivalent to 16,000 ISO), Hi0.7 (20,000 ISO), and Hi1.0 (25,600 ISO). Here, noise is unquestionably obvious and you'll probably want to use these settings only as a last resort. You can go even higher using Night Vision in the Effects modes (*page 50*).

› Auto-ISO

By default, the D5300 sets the ISO automatically. It's possible to change to a manual setting in most exposure modes (except 🄰, 🚫, and 🔲). This new setting will continue to apply if you switch exposure modes. However, if you switch to P, S, A, or M mode and then back to a Scene or Effects mode, the camera reverts to Auto-ISO. The D5300 only permanently "remembers" manual settings in P, S, A, or M modes.

The ISO sensitivity settings item in the Shooting menu has a sub-menu called Auto ISO sensitivity control. This is only available in P, S, A, and M modes. If you set this to **On**, you can still manually select an ISO setting, but the D5300 will automatically override this if it determines that this is required for correct exposure. Extra options within this menu allow you to limit the maximum ISO and minimum shutter speed which the camera can employ when applying Auto ISO sensitivity control. For instance, if ISO 3200 produces too much image noise for your liking, you can set the Auto-ISO limit to 1600.

› Setting the ISO

The usual way to set the ISO is through the Active Information Display:

1) Select the **ISO** item and press (OK) to reveal a list of options.

2) Use the Multi-selector to highlight the required setting, then press (OK) to accept it. Alternatively, use the **ISO sensitivity settings** item in the Shooting menu. A third option is available. You can assign the **Fn** button to **ISO sensitivity** in Custom setting f1 (*see page 119*); in fact, this is the default setting. At this setting,

pressing **Fn** highlights **ISO** in the Information Display; keep it pressed and you can change the setting simply by rotating the Command Dial. If you change ISO settings regularly (and arguably you should!), this is the fastest way to do so and probably the best use of the **Fn** button.

LOW ISO ⌄
As I was using a tripod anyway, I set the ISO to its lowest value to maximize dynamic range. *18mm, 30 sec., f/11, ISO 100.*

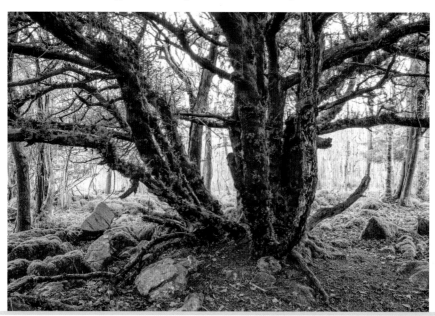

› Working with ISO

Variable ISO is one of the greatest advantages of digital over film, as you'll appreciate if you've ever struggled with a 35mm camera and the wrong speed film. Being able to vary the ISO at any time gives terrific flexibility and many digital photographers change it almost as often as they do aperture and shutter speed.

HIGH ISO ≫

This cyclocross event took place on a fairly dull day and to add to the challenge this part of the course was heavily shaded by trees. Competitors were moving relatively slowly on the climb but I still needed to keep the shutter speed fairly high, and this dictated a high ISO rating. Fortunately image quality remains excellent. *150mm, 1/400 sec., f/4, ISO 1000.*

GO WITH THE FLOW ≫

I used a low ISO and a small aperture mainly to allow a slow shutter speed to smooth the flow of the water. *12mm, ¹/₃ sec., f/22, ISO 100, tripod.*

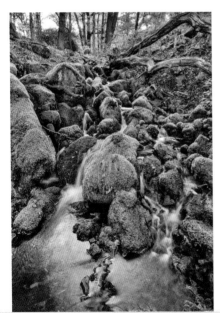

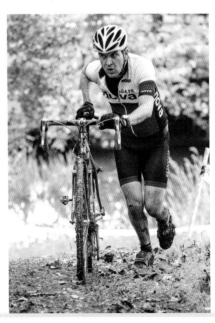

2 » TWO-BUTTON RESET

You can reset a large number of settings (below) to default values. Hold down MENU and 🖲 (marked with green dots) together for at least 2 sec. *See page 23.*

Item	Default setting	
Image quality	JPEG Normal	
Image size	Large	
Release mode	Single frame (Continuous H in 🐾 and 🐕)	
ISO sensitivity	Auto, Scene, and Effects modes	Auto
	User-control modes	100
White balance	Auto (fine tuning off)	
Nikon Picture Controls	Resets any modifications to current Picture Control	
Autofocus mode	AF-A (except 🏃, see page 50)	
Autofocus mode (Live View)	AF-S	
AF-Area mode	🌷, 🔆, 🍴, 🏞, Hi, Lo	Single-point ([ ])
	🏃, 🐕	Dynamic Area
	P, S, A, M, 📷AUTO, 🚫, 🎆, 🏞, 🎇, 🎭, 🌆, 🌃, 🎪, 🎨, 🍷, ✏, 📷⊕, 📷, TOY, 🖥	Auto-area (▣)
AF-Area mode (Live View/ movie shooting)	📷AUTO, 🚫, 🎆, 🏞, 🎇, 🌆, 🌃, 🎪, 🎨, 🍷, ✏, 🔆	Face-priority (😊)
	P, S, A, M, 🏃, 🎭, 🐕, 🏃, 🖌, 🕯, 📷⊕, 🏞, Hi, Lo, TOY, 🖥	Wide-area
	🌷, 🍴	Normal-area
Focus point	Center	
Metering	Matrix	
AE/AF lock hold	Off	
Active D-Lighting	Auto	
Flexible program	Off	
Exposure compensation	Off	
Flash compensation	Off	
HDR mode	Off	
Multiple exposure	Off	
Bracketing	Off	
Flash mode	📷AUTO, 🎆, 🌷, 🎇, 🐕, 🕯, TOY	Auto
	🌆	Auto slow sync
	🎭	Auto with red-eye reduction
	P, S, A, M	Front-curtain sync

» LIVE VIEW

Until recently, Live View on a DSLR has been seen an adjunct to the Viewfinder, not a substitute for it. The SLR is essentially designed around the Viewfinder and it still has many advantages for general picture-taking: it's more intuitive and offers the sense of a direct connection to the subject, and the risk of camera shake is much reduced. Viewfinder-based autofocus is very much faster, so the Viewfinder is often the only realistic option for action shooting.

However, attitudes are changing. To get the full benefit from the high image quality of today's cameras, discerning shooters use tripods regularly; this dilutes the handling advantages of the Viewfinder. Also, Live View focusing, though much slower than Viewfinder-based AF, is more accurate. Live View also gives you a form of depth of field preview (*see page 59*), which the Viewfinder doesn't offer.

Finally, Live View is the jumping-off point for shooting movies, so familiarity with Live View is helpful if you're new to video shooting.

› Using Live View

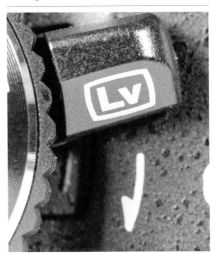

LIVE VIEW ACTIVATION SWITCH ◂

To activate Live View, pull back and release the ⟨Lv⟩ switch on top of the camera, by the Mode Dial. To exit Live View, pull and release again.

The mirror flips up, the Viewfinder blacks out, and the LCD screen displays a continuous live preview of the scene. A range of shooting information is displayed at the top and bottom of the screen, partly overlaying the image. Pressing **INFO** changes this information display, cycling through a series of screens as shown in the table below. A further press returns to the starting screen.

2

When Live View is active, pressing
⏺ superimposes a modified Active
Information Display on the screen and
you can select options in the usual way.
Press ⏺ again, or press the shutter, to
hide this display.

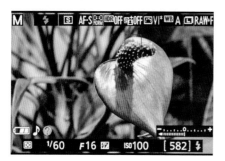

SHOW DETAILED PHOTO INDICATORS ⌃

Press the shutter-release button fully to
take a picture, as in normal shooting. In
the continuous release modes the mirror
stays up, and the monitor remains blank,
between shots, making it almost impossible

to follow moving subjects (another reason
why shooting with the Viewfinder is better
for action).

If Auto or Scene modes are selected,
exposure control is fully automatic, except
that in Scene modes exposure level can be
locked by pressing and holding *AE-L/AF-L*. In
P, S, A, or M modes, exposure control is
much the same as in normal shooting.
If you use exposure compensation in P, S,
or A modes, the brightness of the Live
View display changes to reflect this.
However, this can't be relied on as a
preview of the final image. In M mode
the brightness of the display does not
change as you adjust settings.

Live View info	Details
Show detailed photo indicators (default)	Information bars superimposed at top and bottom of screen.
Show movie indicators	Information for movie shooting superimposed; movie frame area also indicated (*see page 175*); pressing ⏺ brings up movie-related options.
Hide indicators	Screen clear of all information.
Framing grid	Grid lines appear, useful for critical framing.
Show basic photo indicators	Key shooting information shown at bottom of screen.

› Focusing in Live View

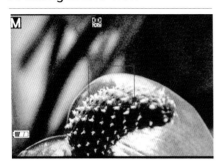

FOCUSING IN LIVE VIEW ⌃
The focus area (red rectangle) can be positioned anywhere on screen, and you can also zoom in for greater precision.

Focusing in Live View operates differently from normal shooting—because the mirror is locked up, the usual focusing

sensor is unavailable. Instead, the camera reads focus information directly from the main image sensor. This is slower than normal AF operation—often very noticeably so—but very accurate. You can also zoom in the view, which helps in placing the focus point exactly where you want it—and in manual focusing too.

Live View has its own set of autofocus options, with two AF modes and four AF-area modes.

Live View AF modes

The AF-mode options are **Single-servo AF (AF-S)** and **Full-time servo AF (AF-F)**. AF-S corresponds to AF-S in normal shooting: the camera focuses when the shutter release is pressed halfway, and maintains that focus if you hold *AE-L/AF-L*

AF Mode	Description
🔲 **Face priority**	Uses face detection to identify people. Yellow border appears outlining faces. If multiple subjects are detected, the camera focuses on the closest. Default in most Scene modes.
Wide-area	Camera analyzes focus information from area approximately $1/6$ the width and height of the frame; area is shown by red rectangle. Default in 🌷 and 🍴.
Normal area	Camera analyzes focus information from a much smaller area, shown by red rectangle. Useful for precise focusing on small subjects. Default in 🏃, 🖼, 🐱, 🏔, 🔆, 🔅.
⊞ **Subject tracking**	Camera follows selected subject as it moves within the frame. Not available in 🏔, 🌙, 🖌, 🧸.

(except in and). AF-F corresponds roughly to AF-C in normal shooting. However, the camera continues to seek focus as long as Live View remains active. When you press the shutter-release button halfway, the focus will lock, and remains locked until you release the button or take a shot.

Selecting the Live View AF mode

1) Activate Live View with the Lv switch.

2) Press ꞏꞏꞏ to engage the Active Information Display and use the Focus mode item to select between AF-S and AF-F (Manual Focus is also available).

3) Press ꞏꞏꞏ again to return to Live View.

Live View AF-area mode

AF-area modes determine how the focus point is selected. There are four Live View AF-area modes, which are different from those used in normal shooting (see below). Again, selection is through the Active Information Display—except in ꞏ, ꞏ, and ꞏ, where AF-area mode is predetermined.

› Using Live View AF

Wide-area AF and Normal area AF

In both these AF modes, you can move the focus point (outlined in red) anywhere on the screen, using the Multi-selector in the usual way. Pressing 🔍 zooms the screen view—press repeatedly to zoom closer. Helpfully, the zoom centers on the focus point. This allows ultra-precise focus control, especially when shooting on a tripod; it's excellent for macro

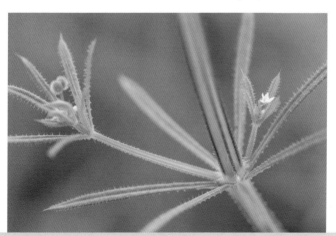

NORMAL «
AREA AF
Normal area AF is the best choice for precision and accuracy, and well suited to the stringent focusing demands of close-up photography. *100mm macro, 1/250 sec., f/8, ISO 200, tripod.*

photography (*page 160*). Once the focus point is set, autofocus is activated as normal by half-pressing the shutter-release button. The red rectangle turns green when focus is achieved.

Tip

The ability to move the focus point anywhere on screen is useful for off-center subjects, especially when using a tripod. In handheld shooting, it's often quicker and easier to use the Viewfinder and employ focus lock (page 76).

Face-priority AF

When this mode is active, the camera automatically detects up to 35 faces and selects the closest. The selected face is outlined with a double yellow border. You can override this and focus on a different person by using the Multi-selector to shift the focus point. To focus on the selected face, press the shutter-release button halfway.

Subject tracking AF

When Subject tracking is selected, a white rectangle appears at the center of the screen. If necessary, move this to align with the desired subject, using the Multi-selector, then press (OK). The camera "memorizes" the subject and the rectangle

then turns yellow. It will now track the subject as it moves, and can even reacquire the subject if it temporarily leaves the frame. To focus, press the shutter-release button halfway; the target rectangle blinks green as the camera focuses and then becomes solid green. If the camera fails to focus the rectangle blinks red instead. Pictures can still be taken but focus may not be correct. To end focus tracking press (OK) again.

Manual focus

Manual focus is engaged as in normal shooting (*see page 73*). However the Live View display continues to reflect the selected Live View AF mode. It's helpful to have Wide-area AF or Normal-area AF selected.

Warning!

Subject tracking can't keep up with rapidly moving subjects. Viewfinder shooting is much more effective for real action photography.

The D5300's excellent screen makes playback pleasurable as well as informative. To display the most recent image, press ▶ ; if **Image Review** is **On** (selected in the Playback menu), images are also displayed automatically after shooting. (In CH or CL release modes, review begins after the last image in a burst is captured; images are shown in sequence.)

> **Note:**
> To conserve the battery, the monitor turns off after a period of inactivity. The default is 1 min. but intervals of 20 sec. or 5 min. can be set using Custom setting c2.

› Viewing other images

To view other images on the memory card, use ▶ to view images in the order of capture, ◀ to view in reverse order ("go back in time").

› Viewing photo information

A wide range of information about each image can be viewed on playback, using ▲ / ▼ to scroll through up to nine pages of information.

To determine which pages are visible,

visit Playback display options in the Playback menu (see table opposite). After checking or unchecking options, scroll up to **Done** and press (OK) to confirm changes.

› Playback zoom

To assess sharpness, or for other critical viewing, you can zoom in on a section of an image.

1) Press (up to 10 times) to zoom the currently selected image. A small navigation window appears briefly, with a yellow outline indicating the visible area.

2) Use the Multi-selector to view other areas of the image.

3) Rotate the Command Dial to see other images at the same magnification.

4) To return to full-frame viewing, press (OK) .

> **Tip**
>
> *High magnification—the equivalent of 10 presses—appears pixelated and is of debatable value. It can give you the impression that none of your images are properly sharp. Eight presses should be enough even for critical users.*

Playback pages	Selection	Details
File information	Always available	Displays large image; basic file info displayed at bottom of screen.
Overview	On by default; disable from Playback menu	Displays small image, simplified histogram, summary information. Focus point used can also be shown: select using **Playback display options>Focus point**.
None (image only)	Enable from Playback menu	Displays large image with no other data
Location data	Only appears when GPS location data was recorded during shooting (*see page 230*).	
Shooting data (three pages)	Enable from Playback menu	See below
RGB histogram	Enable from Playback menu	See below
Highlights	Enable from Playback menu	See below

› Viewing images as thumbnails

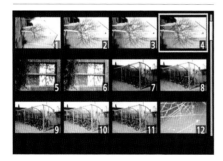

From most screens (not Overview or Highlights), press ⊖▦ to display 4 images; repeat to see 9 or 72 images. Press ⊕ to see fewer. The currently selected image is outlined in yellow.

› Calendar View

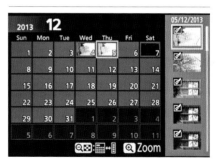

Calendar View displays images grouped by the date on which they were taken. With 72 images displayed, press ⊖▦ again to reach the first calendar page (Date View), with the most recent date highlighted, and pictures from that date in a strip on the right (the thumbnail list). Use the Multi-selector to select other dates. Press ⊖▦ again to enter the thumbnail list so you can scroll through pictures from the selected date; press ⊕ for a larger preview of the selected image.

› Deleting images

To delete the current image, or the selected image in thumbnail view, press 🗑. A confirmation dialog appears. To proceed, press 🗑 again; to cancel, press ▶.

In Calendar View you can also delete all images taken on a selected date. Highlight that date in Date View, then press 🗑; when the confirmation dialog appears press 🗑 again to delete or ▶ to cancel.

› Protecting images

To protect the current image, press **AE-L/AF-L**. To remove protection, press again. Protected images can't be deleted as above, but will be deleted when the memory card is formatted.

› Histogram displays

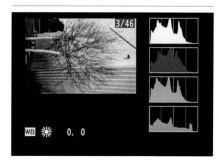

RGB HISTOGRAM

This histogram shows a good spread of tones and there are no spikes at left or right, which would indicate clipping in shadows or highlights (see opposite).

The histogram is a kind of graph showing the distribution of dark and light tones in an image. For assessing whether images are correctly exposed it's much more objective than examining the playback image itself—especially in bright conditions, when it's hard to see the screen image clearly.

The Overview page shows a single histogram; checking **RGB histogram** under **Playback display options** in the Playback menu gives access to a display showing individual histograms for the three color channels (red, green, and blue). The histogram display is a core feature of image playback and usually the page I view first.

› Highlights display

The D5300 can also display a flashing warning for areas of the image with "clipped" highlights, i.e. completely white areas with no detail recorded. This is another useful and objective exposure check.

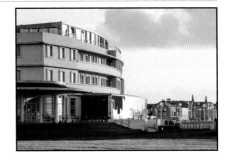

SHINING EXAMPLE ⌄
I wanted the image to sparkle, but knew that if I overexposed even slightly the highlights could merge into larger blank areas, so I checked the highlight display after I took the first shot. *102mm, 1/320 sec., f/14, ISO 200.*

HIGHLIGHTS DISPLAY ⌃
This image is taken from Adobe Lightroom, where the highlights are shown in red—in the display on the camera back these areas would flash black, but this would not show up on a printed page.

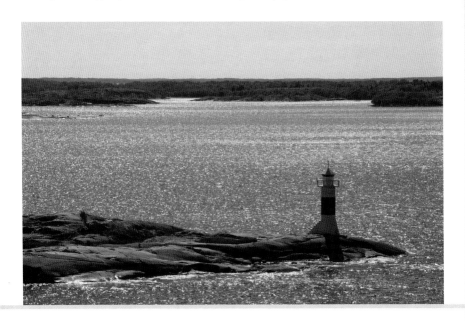

2 » IMAGE ENHANCEMENT

The D5300 offers two main kinds of in-camera image adjustment and enhancement. First, certain settings can be applied before shooting an image (pre-shoot controls).

Second, changes can be made to existing images on the memory card (post-shoot options); access these from the Retouch Menu (*see page 126*).

› Pre-shoot controls

Basic settings like exposure and white balance are crucial for the final image. The D5300 offers several other ways to influence how the image will look, notably with Nikon Picture Controls and Active D-Lighting.

Tip

Picture Controls and Active D-Lighting have a direct effect on JPEG images. When shooting RAW files, they have no effect on the basic raw data. However, they do affect the appearance of preview/playback images, so appropriate settings can still be helpful.

› Active D-Lighting

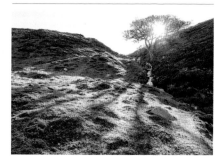

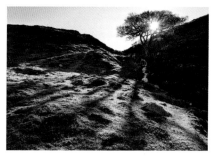

ACTIVE D-LIGHTING COMPARISON ⌃
The shot with ADL Off (top) loses a lot of its impact due to the bleached-out sky. With ADL set to Extra high (above) the image looks darker overall but retains detail into the shadows. *18mm, 1/30 (top) and 1/60 sec., f/10 (top) and f/11, ISO 200.*

Active D-Lighting enhances the D5300's ability to handle scenes with a wide range of brightness (dynamic range). Essentially, it reduces the overall exposure in order to capture more detail in the brightest areas, while mid-tones and shadows are lightened as the camera processes the image. (Don't confuse it with D-Lighting—see page 127—a post-shoot option.)

1) In the Active Information Display, select **ADL** and press ⊙ⓚ. Alternatively, in the Shooting menu, select **Active D-Lighting**.

2) Select from the options to determine the strength of the effect (the default setting is **Auto**). Press ⊙ⓚ.

› ADL bracketing

You can set the camera to take two shots, one with Active D-Lighting off and one with it on, using the current setting (see above).

1) Set Custom setting e6 to **ADL bracketing**.

2) In the Active Information Display, highlight **BKT** (bottom right) and press ⊙ⓚ.

3) Select **ADL** and press ⊙ⓚ.

From here on, alternate shots will be taken with and without Active D-Lighting, until bracketing is cancelled. To cancel, repeat steps 2 and 3, selecting **OFF** in step 3.

› Nikon Picture Controls

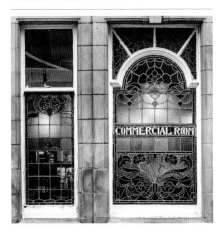

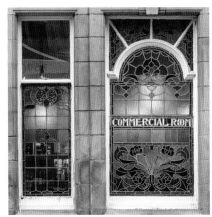

VIVID & NEUTRAL PICTURE CONTROLS ⌃
Vivid (top) and Neutral Picture Controls (above) applied to the same subject. *86mm, 1/125 sec., f/5.3, ISO 1600.*

Picture Controls influence the way JPEG files are processed by the camera. In Auto, Scene, and Effects modes, Picture Controls are predetermined, but in P, S, A, or M modes you can freely choose and fine-tune them.

There are six preset Picture Controls. Names like **Neutral (NL)** and **Vivid (VI)** are self-explanatory, and **Monochrome (MC)** even more so.

Standard (SD) gives a compromise setting which works reasonably well in a wide range of situations. **Portrait (PT)** is designed to deliver milder contrast, saturation, and sharpening, with color balance that is flattering to skin tones. **Landscape (LS)** produces higher contrast and saturation for more vibrant, punchy images.

Selecting Nikon Picture Controls

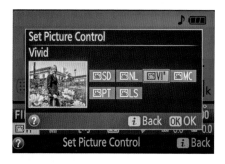

PICTURE CONTROL SELECTION IN THE ACTIVE INFORMATION DISPLAY

1) In the Active Information Display, highlight **Set Picture Control** and press (OK). Alternatively, in the Shooting menu, select **Set Picture Control**.

2) Use the Multi-selector to highlight the required Picture Control and press (OK). This Picture Control will now apply to all images taken in P, S, A, or M modes. Scene/Effects modes continue to apply their preset Picture Controls.

Modifying Picture Controls

You can also modify the standard Nikon Picture Controls to your own taste. Use **Quick Adjust** to make swift, across-the-board changes, or adjust the parameters (such as Sharpening, Contrast) individually.

1) In the Shooting menu, select **Set Picture Control**.

2) Highlight the required Picture Control and press ▶.

3) Use the Multi-selector to select **Quick Adjust** or one of the specific parameters. Use ▶ or ◀ to change each value as desired.

4) When all parameters are as required, press (OK). The new values apply until you modify that Picture Control again.

» MONOCHROME

A Monochrome Picture Control can deliver great results, but you can't convert the image back to color later.

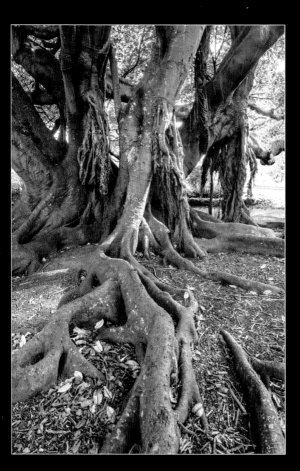

Settings
> ISO 800
> 1/60 sec. at f/8
> 14mm lens

Creating Custom Picture Controls

You can create up to nine additional Picture Controls, either in-camera or using Nikon's Picture Control Utility software (a free download from Nikon websites). Custom Picture Controls can be shared with other Nikon DSLRs. For further details see the *D5300 Reference Manual* and Picture Control Utility's Help menu.

Creating Custom Picture Controls in-camera

1) From the Shooting menu, select **Manage Picture Control**.

2) Select **Save/edit** and press ▶.

3) Highlight an existing Picture Control and press ▶.

4) Edit the Picture Control (as described above). When all parameters are as required, press (OK).

5) On the next screen, name the new Picture Control. By default, its name derives from the original Picture Control on which it is based, plus a two-digit number (e.g. "VIVID-02") but you can create a new name up to 19 characters long. For entering text *see page 124*.

6) Press (OK) to store the new Picture Control. The new Picture Control is now available in P, S, A, or M modes.

› HDR (high dynamic range)

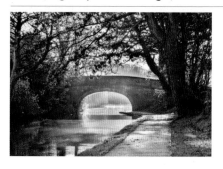

HDR COMPOSITE　　　　　　　　　　☆ ››
An HDR image (above) and two (simulated) source frames: HDR strength was set to High. *70mm, source images 1/320 sec. (center) and 1/30 sec. (right), f/10, ISO 100.*

"Contrast", "dynamic range", and "tonal range" all refer to the range of brightness between the brightest and darkest areas of a scene. Our eyes adjust continuously, allowing us to see detail in both bright areas and deep shade. By comparison, even the best cameras often fall short, losing detail ("clipping") in shadows, highlights or even both.

Shooting RAW gives some chance of recovering highlight and/or shadow detail in post-processing. Active D-Lighting (*page 98*) or D-Lighting (*page 127*) can help with JPEG images. However, all have their limits. Sometimes it's simply impossible to capture the entire brightness range of a scene in a single exposure. Both the histogram display (*page 96*) and the

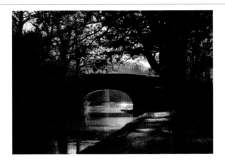

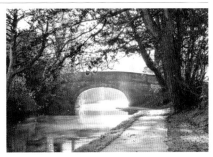

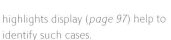

highlights display (*page 97*) help to identify such cases.

When the brightness range does exceed what the camera can capture in a single shot, one possible solution is to shoot more than one exposure and then combine the results. The D5300 can automate this, creating a high dynamic range JPEG image by merging two separate shots taken at different exposures, one biased towards the shadows and one towards the highlights.

1) Select **HDR** in the Active Information Display. It is only available when Image Quality is set to JPEG (not RAW+JPEG).

2) Select **On** and press ▶. If you shoot HDR regularly you can assign **Fn** to this function (Custom setting f1). You can also access HDR from the Shooting menu.

3) Choose the strength of the effect. **Auto** allows the camera to determine this

automatically, or you can select **Low**, **Normal**, **High**, or **Extra High**.

4) Shoot as normal. Because two exposures are made, it's a good idea to use a tripod or some other solid support. Results with moving subjects may appear odd; try Active D-Lighting instead.

5) The camera automatically shoots two images in quick succession. It then takes a few seconds to combine them and display the results. During this interval **Job Hdr** appears in the Viewfinder and you can't take further shots.

6) HDR shooting is automatically cancelled. To shoot more HDR images, repeat the process from step 1.

You can take photographs without a lens, even without a camera, but not without light. Light is the essence of photography, so it follows that paying attention to light is vital for a photographer. And light varies in so many ways: intensity, direction, color, and so on.

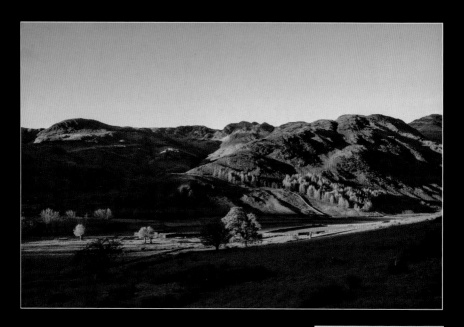

MORNING LIGHT

This is classic side lighting, with the direction of the sunlight almost exactly perpendicular to the direction in which the camera's pointing. In fact, shadows occupy more of the image than sunlit areas, but it just makes the sunlit parts stand out even more.

Settings
> ISO 100
> 1/125 sec. at f/11
> 22mm lens

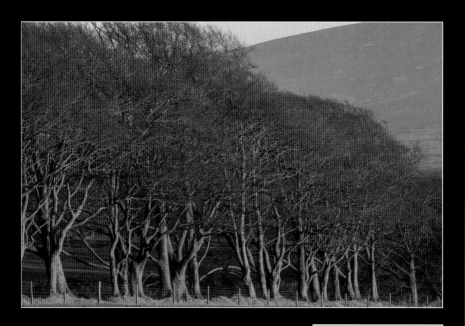

EVENING LIGHT

In some ways the lighting here is similar to the previous picture: low-angled and almost perpendicular to the camera's direction. However, the overwhelming impression is of color, with the typically warm light of the low sun accentuated by the colder tones of the shadows.

Settings
> ISO 250
> 1/60 sec. at f/13
> 125mm lens

3   MENUS

The options that you can access through buttons and dials are only the tip of the iceberg. There are many more ways in which you can customize the D5300 to suit you, but these are only revealed by delving into the menus. There are six of these: Playback, Shooting, Custom Setting, Setup, Retouch, and My Menu/Recent Settings.

The **Playback menu**, outlined in blue, covers functions related to playback, including viewing and deleting images. The **Shooting menu**, outlined in green, is used to control shooting settings (many also accessible via the Active Information Display), such as ISO, White Balance, or Active D-Lighting. The **Custom Setting menu**, outlined in red, lets you fine-tune and personalize many aspects of the camera's operation. The **Setup menu**, outlined in orange, governs a range of functions such as LCD brightness, plus others that you may need to change only rarely, such as language and time settings. The **Retouch menu**, outlined in purple, lets you create modified copies of images on the memory card. Finally **My Menu**, outlined in gray, is a handy place to store

items from other menus that you use frequently, and can also become a Recent Settings menu.

Navigating the menus

1) To display the main menu screen, press **MENU**.

2) Scroll up or down with the Multi-selector to highlight the different menus. To enter the desired menu, press ▶.

3) Scroll up or down with the Multi-selector to highlight specific menu items. To select an item, press ▶. In most cases this will take you to a further set of options.

4) Scroll up or down with the Multi-selector to choose the desired setting. To select, press ▶ or ⓞⓚ. In some cases you may need to scroll up to **Done** and then press ⓞⓚ to make changes effective.

5) To return to the previous screen, press ◀. To exit the menus completely without effecting any changes, semi-depress the shutter-release button.

> ### Tip
>
> *You can access help from within the menus by pressing ⊖. Help information is available when a ? icon appears in the bottom left corner of the monitor.*

» PLAYBACK MENU

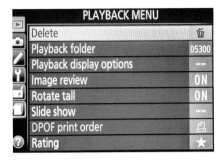

The D5300's Playback menu contains nine different items which affect how images are viewed, stored, shared, deleted, and printed. Most of these are only accessible when a memory card—with image(s)—is present in the camera.

› Delete

This function allows images stored on the memory card to be deleted, either singly or in batches.

1) In the Playback menu, highlight **Delete** and press ►.

2) In the menu options screen, choose **Selected**, **Select date**, **or All**.

3) If you choose **Selected**, images in the active playback folder or folders (see next page) are displayed as thumbnail images. Use the Multi-selector to scroll through the displayed images. Press and hold ⊕ to view the highlighted image full-screen. Press ⊖ to mark the highlighted shot for deletion (you might think you'd use 🗑, but you can't). The image will be tagged with a 🗑 icon. If you change your mind, highlight a tagged image and press ⊖ again to remove the tag. Repeat this process to select further images. Press (OK) to see a confirmation screen. Select **YES** and press (OK) to delete the selected image(s); to exit without deleting any images, select **NO**.

4) If you choose **Select date**, you'll see a list of dates on which images on the memory card were taken. Use the Multi-selector to scroll through the list. Press ► to mark the highlighted date for deletion. It will be checked in the list. If you change your mind, highlight the date and press ► again to remove the tag. Repeat this procedure to select further dates. Press (OK) to see a confirmation screen. Select **YES** and press (OK) to delete all image(s) taken on the selected date(s); to exit without deleting any images, select **NO**.

3

Tip

Individual images can also be deleted from the normal playback screen, and this is usually more convenient (see page 96).

› Playback folder

By default, the D5300's playback screen will only display images in the current folder. For most of us, there is only ever one folder on the memory card, so this is of no significance. However, if you're one of the few who does end up with multiple folders, you can view images in all folders by changing this setting from **Current** to **All**.

Note:
The current folder is chosen through the Shooting menu (*see page 111*).

› Playback display options

This is an important menu, as it enables you to choose what (if any) information about each image will be displayed on playback, over and above the bare-bones info screen that is always available. As such, these options have already been described on *page 94*.

› Image review

If Image review is **On**, the latest image is automatically displayed on the monitor immediately after shooting. If **Off**, images are only displayed when you press ▶. If you're looking to eke out longer battery life, choose **Off**.

› Rotate tall

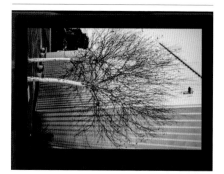

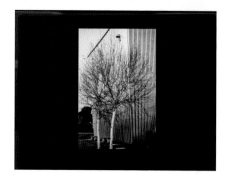

ROTATE TALL OFF AND ON   ⌃

This determines whether portrait format ("tall") images are displayed the "right way up" during playback/image review. If set to **Off**, which is the default, these images will not be rotated, meaning that you need to turn the camera through 90° to view them correctly. If set to **On**, these images will be correctly orientated. However, because the monitor screen is rectangular, they will appear smaller.

› Slide show

Enables you to display images as a slide show, either on the camera's screen or when it is connected to a TV. All images in the folder or folders selected for playback (under the Playback Folder menu) will be played in chronological order.

1) Make sure the playback screen is set to Image only (*see page 95*) to ensure an uncluttered slide show.

2) In the Playback menu, select **Slide show**.

3) Select **Image type** (i.e. still images, movies, or both). You can also select **By rating** to, for example, only include images you've rated five stars (*see page 110* for more on rating images).

4) Select **Frame interval.** Choose between **2**, **3**, **5**, or **10** seconds. Press (OK).

5) Select **Start** and press (OK).

6) When the show ends, a dialog screen is displayed. Select **Restart** and press (OK) to play again. Select **Frame interval** and press (OK) to return to the Frame interval dialog. Select **Exit** and press (OK) to exit.

7) If you press (OK) during the slide show, the slide show is paused and the same screen displayed. The only difference is that if you select **Restart** and press (OK), the show will resume where it left off.

› DPOF print order

This allows you to select JPEG image(s) to be printed when the camera is connected to, or the memory card is inserted into, a printer that complies with the DPOF (Digital Print Order Format) standard. If there are no JPEG images on the memory card this menu item is unavailable. For more on printing see Chapter 9, *page 231*.

1) In the Playback menu, highlight **Print set (DPOF)** and press ▶.

2) In the next screen, choose **Select/set.** Images in the current playback folder are displayed as thumbnails.

3) Use ▶/◀ to scroll through the displayed images. Press and hold ⊕ to view the highlighted image full-screen.

4) Press ▲ to select the image to be printed as a single copy. It will be tagged with a 🖶 icon and the number "01". To print more than one copy, press ▲ as many times as necessary; the number displayed increases accordingly.

5) Repeat this procedure to select further images. When all desired images have been selected, press (OK).

6) From the confirmation screen select **Print shooting data** if you wish shutter speed and aperture to be shown on all pictures printed. Select **Print date** if you wish the date of the photo to be shown. When you're ready to confirm the order, press (OK).

> ## Rating

This allows you to assign images a rating from one to five stars—and we've just seen, in **Slide show**, one possible use for this feature.

To assign ratings
1) In the Playback menu, highlight **Rating** and press ▶. Images in the current Playback folder are displayed as thumbnails.

2) Use ▶/◀ to scroll through the displayed images. Press and hold ⊕ to view the highlighted image full-screen. Use ▲ to

assign the image up to five stars (use ▼ to reduce a rating).

3) Repeat with further images. When finished, press (OK) to exit.

> ## Select to send to smart device

This allows you to select existing images to be uploaded to your smartphone or tablet when you connect through Nikon's Wireless Mobile Utility (*see page 224*).

1) In the Playback menu, highlight **Select to send to smart device** and press ▶. Images in the current playback folder are displayed as thumbnails.

2) Use the Multi-selector to scroll through the displayed images. Press and hold ⊕ to see a larger version of the highlighted image. Press ⊖▦ to select the highlighted shot for upload. The image will be tagged with a ▶ icon. If you change your mind, highlight a tagged image and press ⊖▦ again to remove the tag.

3) Repeat this process to select further images. When satisfied, press (OK) to exit.

» SHOOTING MENU

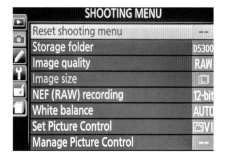

The Shooting menu contains numerous options, but many of these are also accessible through the Active Information Display and have already been discussed.

› Reset shooting menu

This is simply a quick way to restore Shooting menu settings to the camera's original default settings. Use with caution as it can wipe out settings that you have carefully created.

1) In the Shooting menu, select **Reset shooting menu** and press (OK).

2) Select **Yes** and press (OK). Or select **No** to make no changes.

› Storage folder

By default the D5300 stores images in a single folder (named "100D5300"). If multiple memory cards are used they will all end up holding folders of the same name. This isn't usually a problem but a few users might wish to avoid it. You might also want to create specific folders for different shoots or different types of image.

The camera will automatically create a new folder when the current one becomes full. "Full" means it contains 999 images. If you download to your computer regularly and then format the card for reuse, this may never happen. However, it is a possibility if you are very prolific or you're travelling for long periods without access to a computer. In this case you might prefer to create an ordered series of folders, perhaps organized by location or date.

To create a new folder
1) In the Shooting menu, select **Storage folder** and press ▶.

2) Select New and press ▶.

3) Name the folder. The first three digits are assigned automatically, so only five (letters or numbers) are available. For details on text entry, see **Image comment**, *page 124*.

4) When you've set the name, press (OK) to create the new folder. It automatically becomes the active folder.

You can also **Rename** an existing folder using a similar process.

To change the active folder

1) In the Shooting menu, select **Select folder** and press ▶.

2) Scroll through the list (assuming more than one folder exists) and press (OK) to select a folder.

› Image quality

Use this to choose between NEF (RAW) and JPEG options, as described on *page 79*.

› Image size

Use this to select image size, as described on *page 80*. If RAW is selected for Image quality this item is grayed out and cannot be accessed.

› NEF (RAW) recording

This menu offers allows you to set **NEF (RAW) bit depth** to either **12-bit** or **14-bit**. *See page 78*.

› White balance

Allows you to set the white balance, discussed in depth on *page 82*.

› Set Picture Control and Manage Picture Control

These menus govern the use of Nikon Picture Controls, discussed in depth on *page 99*.

› Auto distortion control

If **On**, this automatically corrects for distortion (*see page 192*) which may arise with certain lenses. It's available only with Type G and D lenses (*see page 184*), excluding fisheye and PC lenses, and only affects JPEG images. Distortion affecting RAW images can only be dealt with in post-processing.

› Color space

Allows you to choose between sRGB and Adobe RGB color spaces (*see page 84*).

› Active D-Lighting

Governs the use of Active D-Lighting, discussed in depth on *page 98*.

› HDR (high dynamic range)

Enable and control HDR shooting, as described on *page 102*.

› High ISO NR

Photos taken at high ISO settings can also be marred by increased "noise". The default setting of **Normal** applies a middling level of NR. This can be changed to **Low** or **High**. It can also be set to **Off**, but light-touch NR is still applied to JPEG images taken at ISO 1250 or above.

> ### *Tip*
>
> *High levels of NR will remove most noise but can "smooth" the image so much it looks "plastic" and loses any semblance of fine detail. And with JPEG images, you can't restore any of the lost texture or detail. Unless you're in a hurry, it's better to apply noise-reduction in post-processing, when you can see the effect more clearly and back off if necessary.*

› Long exposure NR

Photos taken at long shutter speeds can suffer from increased "noise" and the D5300 therefore offers the option of extra image processing to counteract this. If Long exposure noise reduction (its full name) is **On**, it applies at exposure times of 1 sec. or longer. During image processing, **Job nr** flashes in the Viewfinder. The time

taken is roughly equal to the shutter speed in use, and no further pictures can be taken until processing is complete. This causes significant delays in shooting and many users prefer to use post-processing to reduce image noise. For this reason, Long exp. NR is **Off** by default.

› ISO sensitivity settings

This menu governs ISO sensitivity settings, discussed in depth on *page 85*.

› Release mode

This menu governs release mode options, and offers the same choices as using ⏣ and the Active Information Display (*see page 32*).

› Multiple exposure

When you can merge images on the computer, precisely and flexibly, it might seem that cameras like the D5300 hardly need a multiple exposure facility. However, the Nikon manual states "multiple exposures produce colors noticeably superior to those in software-generated photographic overlays." It's debatable whether this would apply if you shot individual RAW images for careful post-processing before merging them on the computer, but clearly this feature does offer an effective way to combine images for immediate use, such as JPEG files for printing.

To create a multiple exposure

1) In the Shooting menu, select **Multiple exposure** and press ▶. Select **On** and press (OK).

2) Select **Number of shots** and use ▲/▼ to choose 2 or 3, then press (OK).

3) Select **Auto gain** and choose **On** or **Off** (see below) then press (OK).

4) Frame the photo and shoot normally.

5) Multiple exposure shooting is automatically reset to **Off**, so you must repeat the whole process if you want to shoot another multiple exposure.

If release mode is CL (Continuous Low speed) or CH (Continuous High speed), the designated images will be exposed in a single burst. In Single Frame release mode, one image in the sequence will be exposed each time you press the shutter-release button. Normally the maximum interval between shots is 30 sec. You can extend this by setting a longer standby time in Custom setting c2. Multiple exposure can also be combined with the camera's Interval timer facility (see below) to take the exposures at set intervals.

Auto gain

Auto gain (**On** by default) adjusts the exposure, so that if you are shooting a sequence of three shots, each is exposed at $^1/_3$ the exposure value required for a normal exposure. You might turn Auto gain **Off** where a moving subject is well lit but the background is dark, to ensure that the subject is well-exposed and the background isn't over-lightened.

› Interval timer shooting

The D5300 can take a number of shots at pre-determined intervals. If **Multiple exposure** is activated first, they will be combined into a single image, otherwise they will be recorded individually.

1) In the Shooting menu, highlight **Interval timer shooting** and press ▶ or (OK).

2) Choose a start time. If you select **Now**, shooting begins 3 sec. after you complete the other settings, and you can skip step 3. For a later starting time, select **Start time** then press ▶ to continue to the next step.

3) Use ◀ and ▶ to select hours or minutes. Use ▲ and ▼ to select the time (in the next 24 hours). Press ▶ to continue to the next step.

4) Choose the interval between shots. Use

◀ and ▶ to select hours, minutes, or seconds. Use ▲ and ▼ to change these values as desired. Press ▶ to continue to the next step.

5) Choose the number of intervals (up to 999) and the number of shots to be taken at each interval (up to 9). The total number of shots that this amounts to is also displayed. Press ▶ to complete the setup and reach the primary Interval timer shooting screen.

6) Highlight **Start> On** and press (OK). If you want to cancel an interval timer sequence before the end, there are several options. The simplest is just to turn the camera off and on again.

> **Note:**
> If you're planning a large number of shots, and/or long intervals, ensure that the battery is fully charged or the camera is connected to a mains adaptor, and that there is sufficient space on the memory card. If the card becomes full during an Interval timer sequence, shooting stops until the card is replaced.

› Movie settings

Sets key options for movie shooting: *see page 170.*

» CUSTOM SETTING MENU

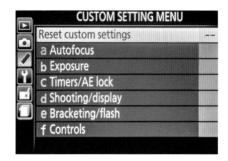

The Custom Setting menu allows you to fine-tune almost every aspect of the camera's operation to suit your personal preferences. There are six subdivisions, identified by key letters and colors: **a: Autofocus** (red); **b: Metering/Exposure** (yellow); **c: Timers/AE Lock** (green); **d: Shooting/display** (light blue); **e: Bracketing/flash** (dark blue) and **f: Controls** (lilac). In addition there is an option to **Reset custom settings**, which restores all current Custom Settings to standard default values.

Navigating the Custom Setting menu is essentially the same as the other menus. However, from the main menu screen, the first press on ▶ takes you into the list of sub-menus. Scroll through these to the desired group and press ▶ to see its constituent items.

Although the menu is organized into seven main groups, individual items do appear as a continuous list, so you can scroll straight down from a4 to b1, and so on. If you scroll up you can go from a1 to f5.

The Custom Setting identifier code (e.g. c2) is shown in the appropriate color for that group. If the setting has been changed from default values, an asterisk appears over the initial letter of the code.

> ### Tip
>
> *If there are certain Custom Settings that you visit frequently, these may be more rapidly accessible via Recent Settings; alternatively, you can opt for My Menu and add them to the list there (see page 135).*

› a: Autofocus

a1 AF-C priority selection

Normally, in AF-C (Continuous-servo) release mode, the camera can only take a picture once focus is acquired (**focus priority**). Custom setting a1 allows you to choose **release priority** instead, meaning that pictures can be taken even if perfect focus has not been acquired. It's up to you whether you think that an out-of-focus shot is better than no shot.

a2 Number of focus points

This governs the number of focus points which you can choose from when selecting

the focus point manually (*see page 76*). By default it uses the full 39 points (**AF39**) but you can also opt to use 11 points (**AF11**). Using the smaller number can speed up the selection process.

> **Note:**
> Even when you select **AF11**, the camera still uses all 39 points for automatic selection, focus tracking, and so on.

a3 Built-in AF-assist illuminator

This determines whether the AF-assist illuminator (*see page 77*) operates when lighting is poor: options are **On** (default) or **Off**.

a4 Rangefinder

This allows you to use the exposure display for assistance in manual focusing (*see page 74*). The default setting is **Off**.

› b: Metering/Exposure

b1 EV steps for exposure cntrl

This governs the increments which the camera uses for setting shutter speed and aperture, as well as for bracketing, and so on. The options are $^1/_3$ **step** (default) or $^1/_2$ **step**.

c1 Shutter-release button AE-L

This determines whether you can lock exposure by half-pressure on the shutter-release button. By default, this item is **Off**, which means that half-pressure locks focus only (see Focus lock, *page 76*), and you can only lock exposure with the *AE-L/AF-L* button. Change it to **On**, and half-pressure locks both focus and exposure.

c2 Auto off timers

Governs the interval before the relevant displays turn off when idle. A shorter delay improves battery life. The displays do not turn off automatically when the D5300 is connected to a computer.

The options you can select are **Short**, **Medium**, or **Long**; these set different intervals for different camera functions (see the table below). **Short** is a good choice if you want to economize battery life. You can also set your own Custom intervals for each of these timers.

c3 Self-timer

This menu has two sub-menus governing the operation of the self-timer.

Self-timer delay determines the interval between pressing the button and the shot being taken. The default is 10 sec., alternatives are 2, 5, and 20 sec.

As well as taking a single shot, you can create sequences from one press of the release button. Number of shots can be set anywhere from 1 to 9; if you set any value larger than 1, the interval between successive shots is approximately 4 sec.

c4 Remote on Duration (ML-L3)

If you're using the optional ML-L3 remote control (*see page 212*), this governs how long the camera will remain on standby for a signal from the remote before remote control mode turns off. Options range from 1 min (default) to 15 min. This does not apply in Live View shooting.

Custom Setting c2 Auto off timers

Interval for:	Short	Normal	Long
Playback/menus	20 sec.	1 min.	5 min.
Image review	4 sec.	4 sec.	20 sec.
Live view	5 min.	10 min.	20 min.
Standby timer	4 sec.	8 sec.	1 min.

d1 Beep

If you wish, the camera can emit a beep when the self-timer operates, and to signify that focus has been acquired when shooting in single-servo AF mode. You can choose a **High** or **Low** pitch for the beep or turn the darn thing **Off** entirely.

d2 Viewfinder grid display

This allows the camera to display grid lines in the Viewfinder—these can help you keep the camera level and assist with precise framing. The options are **Off** (default) and **On**. It's a personal choice, but I always enable the grid on any camera I'm using.

d3 ISO display

By default, this item is **Off**, which means that the figure at bottom right of both the LCD screen and the Viewfinder display shows how many more exposures can be accommodated on the memory card at current Image Size, Area, or Quality settings. Alternatively, you can choose to display the current ISO sensitivity setting instead: set this item to **On**.

d4 File number sequence

This controls how image numbers are set. If it's **Off**—which is the default—file numbering is reset to 0001 whenever you insert a new memory card, format an existing card, or create a new storage folder (*see page 111*). If it's **On**, numbering continues from the previous highest number used; this may help you to manage the images on your computer. Reset creates a new folder and begins numbering from 0001.

> **Note:**
> Even if sequence numbering is **On**, numbering does reset to 0001 after you've shot 9999 images.

d5 Exposure delay mode

You can use this setting to create a delay of approximately 1 sec. when you press the shutter-release button. This is a possible alternative to the self-timer or mirror lock-up to reduce vibration when shooting on a tripod. It's **Off** by default.

d6 Print date

This allows you to imprint Date or Date and time on photos (JPEG only) as they are taken. Date counter imprints number of days to or from a selected date.

> **Note:**
> Date and time information is always embedded in metadata (*see page 226*), without needing to mar the image itself.

› e: Bracketing/flash

e1 Flash cntrl for built-in flash

This governs how the built-in flash is regulated. The default is **TTL**, which means flash output is regulated automatically by the camera's metering system. If you select **Manual** instead, you can press ▶ and use a sub-menu to determine the strength of the flash, from **Full** down to **1/128** power.

e2 Auto bracketing set

Bracketing means taking a sequence of shots while varying certain settings, most commonly those relating to exposure. This has already been discussed in detail (*see page 68*). The options are: **AE bracketing** (default), **WB bracketing**, and **ADL bracketing**.

› f: Controls

f1 Assign Fn. button

A wide range of functions can be assigned to the **Fn** button. In most cases it's used in conjunction with the Command Dial: pressing **Fn** activates the Active Information Display and highlights the selected setting. Hold in the button and turn the Command Dial to change values for that setting. In practice this becomes the quickest way to change values for your chosen setting, whether it's ISO, white balance, or anything else from the list on *page 120*.

f2 Assign *AE-L/AF-L* button

You can also assign a number of different functions to the ***AE-L/AF-L*** button (*page 121*).

f3 Reverse dial rotation

This reverses the effect of rotating the Command Dial in a given direction. For instance, in A mode, turning it to the right normally makes the aperture smaller but you can make it have the opposite effect.

You can customize this separately for **Exposure compensation** and for **Shutter speed/aperture** settings.

f4 Slot empty release lock

By default (i.e. **LOCK** is selected in this menu), the shutter can't be released unless there's a memory card in the camera. The obvious lack of response protects you against shooting away happily for hours, only to discover later that none of your images have been recorded.

Alternatively you can select **ON**. Images are held in the camera's buffer and can be displayed on the monitor (demo mode), but are not recorded.

f5 Reverse indicators

This governs how the exposure displays in the Viewfinder and Information Display are shown. By default (**−0+** selected), over-exposure is indicated by bars on the right side. **+0−** reverses this so overexposure is on the left. There's no reason to change this setting other than personal preference.

3

Custom Setting f1 Assign Fn button

QUAL	Hold button and rotate Command Dial to select image quality/size.	All modes
ISO sensitivity (default)	Hold button and rotate Command Dial to select ISO sensitivity.	All modes
White Balance	Hold button and rotate Command Dial to select white balance setting.	P, S, A, or M modes only
Active D-Lighting	Hold button and rotate Command Dial to select Active D-Lighting setting.	P, S, A, or M modes only
HDR	Hold button and rotate Command Dial to choose HDR settings and make next shot an HDR image.	P, S, A, or M modes only; image quality must be set to JPEG
+NEF (RAW)	When Image quality is set to JPEG, records a NEF copy of the next shot taken.	All modes (except 🎨, 🌙, 🏔, ⊕)
BKT	Hold button and rotate Command Dial to choose bracketing increment or toggle 🔲 on and off.	P, S, A, or M modes only
AF-area mode	Hold button and rotate Command Dial to select AF-area mode.	All modes
Viewfinder grid display	Hold button and rotate Command Dial to toggle grid display on and off.	All modes
Wi-Fi	Press button to open Wi-Fi item in Setup menu.	All modes

Custom Setting f2 Assign *AE-L/AF-L* button: Press

Options   AE/AF lock (default)   Pressing ***AE-L/AF-L*** locks both focus and
                                     exposure until next shot is taken.

              AE lock only   Pressing ***AE-L/AF-L*** locks exposure until next shot
                                     is taken.

              AE lock (Hold)   Pressing ***AE-L/AF-L*** locks exposure for all
                                     subsequent shots, until you press the button
                                     again or the standby timer interval (*see page 117*)
                                     runs out.

              AF lock only   Pressing ***AE-L/AF-L*** locks focus until next shot
                                     is taken.

              AF-ON   Pressing ***AE-L/AF-L*** activates focus: focus can't be
                                     activated with half-press on shutter release.

              FV lock   Pressing ***AE-L/AF-L*** locks flash value (built-in and
                                     compatible flashguns only).

              None   Pressing ***AE-L/AF-L*** has no effect.

3 » SETUP MENU

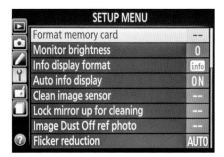

The Setup menu controls various important camera functions, though many are ones you will need to access only occasionally.

› Format memory card

This is the one item in this menu you may use regularly, as it is essential to format any new memory card before use, or one that has been used before in another camera. It is also useful for deleting old images on a card. The process is set out on *page 26*.

› Monitor brightness

This allows you to change the brightness of the LCD display with ▲ / ▼. Use with care; making review/playback images appear brighter does not mean the images themselves (e.g. as viewed on your computer) will be any brighter.

The point of this is to adapt to changing light levels in your surroundings. The

screen shows a "step-wedge" with 10 bands ranging from very dark to very light gray. It should be possible to distinguish clearly between all of them.

> **Note:**
> This does not apply in Live View/ movie shooting: monitor brightness for these is adjusted separately (*see pages 89, 170*).

› Info display format

This lets you choose between **Graphic** (default) and **Classic** modes for the Information Display (*see page 30*). You can also select different background colors for each display mode.

There are separate options for User-control modes (P, S, A, and M) and for Auto, Scene, and Effects modes. Setting a different screen mode, or just a different background color, could be a handy reminder of which group of modes you're in. However, the default for both groups is the same (Graphic mode with blue background).

› Auto info display

By default (i.e. this item is **On**), the Information Display appears automatically when you half-press the shutter-release button. If Image Review is **Off** (*pages 94, 108*), it will also appear immediately after you take a shot.

If you turn this item **Off**, the Information Display only appears when you press **INFO** or ◄🔳►. You can turn it off to save power, or if you're working entirely through the Viewfinder.

› Clean image sensor and Lock mirror up for cleaning

For more details *see page 216*.

› Image Dust Off Ref Photo

Nikon Capture NX2 (*see page 227*) offers automatic removal of dust spots on images by comparing them to a reference photo which maps dust on the sensor. This can save a lot of grunt work compared to manually removing spots from individual images. This menu item allows you to take a suitable reference photo.

To take a dust-off reference photo
1) Fit a CPU lens of at least 50mm focal length. Locate a featureless white object (e.g. a sheet of plain paper), large enough to fill the frame.

2) In the Setup menu, select **Image Dust Off Ref Photo** and press ▶.

3) Select **Start** or **Clean sensor and then start** and press ⊛. (Select **Start** if you have already taken the picture from which you want to remove spots.)

4) Frame the white object at a distance of about 4in. (10cm). Press the shutter-release button halfway; focus is automatically set at infinity. This creates a soft white background against which dust spots stand out clearly.

5) Press the shutter-release button fully to capture the reference image.

› Flicker reduction

Some light sources can produce visible flicker in the Live View screen image and in movie recording. To minimize this, use this menu to match the frequency of the local mains power supply. **60Hz** is common in North America, **50Hz** is normal in the European Union, including the UK. Normally, you can leave this on **Auto** and the camera will adjust automatically.

› Time zone and date

Sets date, time, and time zone, and specifies the date display format (**Y/M/D, M/D/Y**, or **D/M/Y**). Set your home time zone first, then set the time correctly. If you travel to a different time zone, simply set the time zone accordingly and the time will be updated automatically.

> **Note:**
> If the camera's GPS receiver is on, it can correct the clock functions using the very accurate data from the satellite system. See Chapter 9 Connection, *page 230*.

› Language

Set the language which the camera uses in its menus. The options include over 30 European and Asian languages.

› Auto image rotation

If set to **ON** (default), information about the orientation of the camera is recorded with every photo taken, ensuring that they will appear the right way up when viewed with Nikon View NX2/Capture NX2 and most third-party imaging applications. To regulate how photos appear on the camera's own screen, use **Rotate tall** in the Playback menu (*see page 108*).

› Image comment

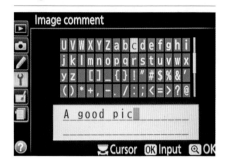

You can append brief comments (36 characters, or about a quarter of a Tweet) to images. Comments appear in the third info page on Playback (*see page 94*) and can be viewed in Nikon View NX2 and Nikon Capture NX2. To attach a comment, select **Input comment** and press ▶.

To enter text, move through the onscreen "keypad" using the Multi-selector. Press **OK** to select the highlighted letter or number and move automatically to the next position. You can also use the Command Dial to move the cursor to a different position. When finished press ⊕. Select **Attach comment**, then select **Done**, and press ⊛. The comment will be attached to all new shots until turned off again.

› Location data

This item regulates the operation of the onboard GPS. See Chapter 9 Connection, *page 230*.

› Video mode

The name is potentially confusing, as this is not directly related to the camera's Movie mode. You can connect the camera to a TV or VCR to view images; this menu sets the camera to **NTSC** or **PAL** standards to match the device you're connecting to. NTSC is used in North America and Japan, but most of the world uses PAL.

› HDMI

You can also connect the camera to HDMI (High Definition Multimedia Interface) TVs—you'll need a special cable. This menu sets the camera's output to match the HDMI device (get this information from that device's specs or instructions). The Device control submenu applies when connected to an HDMI-CEC television, and allows the TV remote to be used to navigate through images.

› Remote control

This contains options which apply when you're using some of Nikon's remote cords and wireless remote controls, although not the ML-L3 (*see page 212*).

The first option is **Remote shutter release**. This determines what happens when you press the release button on the remote. You can set it to **Take photos** or **Record movies**.

The second option is **Assign Fn Button**. If the remote has an Fn button, you can set it to **Same as camera AE-L/AF-L button** (i.e. it serves the function you've selected in Custom setting f2). Alternatively you can select **Live view**, which means that the remote's Fn button starts and stops Live View.

› Wi-Fi

Use this to enable and regulate the onboard WiFi. See Chapter 9 Connection, *page 224*.

› Eye-Fi upload

You can also set up a WiFi network connection using an Eye-Fi card (see Chapter 9 Connection, *page 227*). This menu item is only visible when there's an EyeFi card in the memory card slot.

› Conformity marking

This displays some technical standards with which the camera complies. It's for information only; there are no options to choose.

› Firmware version   » RETOUCH MENU

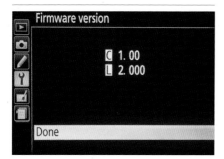

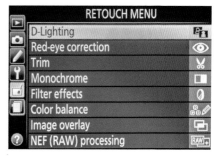

Firmware is the onboard software which controls the camera's operation. Nikon issues updates periodically. This menu shows the version presently installed, so you can verify whether it is current.

When new firmware is released, download it from the Nikon website and copy it to a memory card. Insert this card in the camera then use this menu to update the camera's firmware.

Note:
Firmware updates may include new functions and new menu items, which can make this *Expanded Guide* (and the *Nikon Reference Manual*) appear out of date.

The Retouch menu is used to make corrections and enhancements to images, including cropping, color balance, and much more. This does not affect the original image but creates a copy to which the changes are applied. Further retouching can be applied to the new copy, but you can't apply the same effect twice to the same image.

Copies are always created in JPEG format but the size and quality depends on the format of the original (a few exceptions, such as Trim and Resize, produce copies smaller than the original).

Format of original photo	Quality and size of copy
NEF (RAW)	JPEG (Fine, Large)
JPEG	JPEG (Quality and size match original)

› To create a retouched copy

1) In the Retouch menu, select a retouch option and press ▶. If subsidiary options appear, make a further selection and press ▶ again. A screen of image thumbnails then appears.

2) Select the required image using the Multi-selector, as you would during normal image playback. Press (ok). A preview of the retouched image appears.

3) Depending on the type of retouching to be done (see below), there may be further options to choose from.

4) Press (ok) to create a retouched copy. Or press ◀ to go back to the options screen. To exit without creating a copy, press ▣.

Note:
Retouched copy images are indicated by a ☑ icon in normal image playback.

› Side-by-side comparison

This option is not part of the regular Retouch menu; it is only available in full-frame playback, when a retouched copy, or its source image, is selected. Press ◀❸▶ and

from the next screen select **Retouch** and press ▶. Scroll to **Side-by-side comparison** and press ▶ again.

The screen now shows the copy alongside the original source image. Highlight either image with ◀ or ▶ and press ⊕ to view it full frame. Press ▣ to return to normal playback; to return to the playback screen with the highlighted image selected, press (ok).

› D-Lighting

Though related, D-Lighting should not be confused with Active D-Lighting (*page 98*). Active D-Lighting is applied before shooting, D-Lighting is applied later. In essence, D-Lighing lightens the shadow areas of the image. The D-Lighting screen shows a side-by-side comparison of the original image and a preview of the retouched copy; a press on ⊕ zooms in on this preview. Use ▲ and ▼ to select the strength of the effect, from **Lo** to **Hi**. If your photo contains faces, you can select the **Portrait subjects** box. This will confine the effect to the faces. It will only work if the camera detects faces in the picture, and for three faces at most.

› Red-eye correction

This tackles the notorious problem of "red-eye", caused by on-camera flash (*see page 146*). This option can only be selected for photos taken using flash. The camera analyzes the photo for evidence of red-eye; if none is found the process ends. If red-eye is detected a preview image appears; use the zoom controls and Multi-selector to view it more closely.

› Trim

Crops images to improve framing or to match a specific print size. A preview screen shows the crop area with a yellow rectangle. Change the aspect ratio of the crop with the Command Dial (see the table). Adjust its size using ⊖▦ and ⊕. Shift its position using the Multi-selector.

› Monochrome

Create monochrome copies: straight **Black-and-white**, **Sepia** (a brownish toned effect), or **Cyanotype** (a bluish toned effect). For **Sepia** or **Cyanotype**, you can make the toning effect stronger or weaker with ▲ / ▼.

› Filter effects

Mimics several common photographic filters (perhaps we should say they used to be common in the days of film). **Skylight** reduces the blue cast which can affect photos taken on clear days with a lot of blue sky. Applied to other images its effect is very subtle, even undetectable. **Warm filter** has a much stronger warming effect. **Red**, **green**, and **blue intensifier** are all fairly self-explanatory, as is **Soft**.

Aspect ratio	Possible sizes for trimmed copy									
3:2	5760 x 3840	5120 x 3416	4480 x 2984	3840 x 2560	3200 x 2128	2560 x 1704	1920 x 1280	1280 x 856	960 x 640	640 x 424
4:3	5120 x 3840	4480 x 3360	3840 x 2880	3200 x 2400	2560 x 1920	1920 x 1440	1280 x 960	960 x 720	640 x 480	
5:4	5008 x 4000	4800 x 3840	4208 x 3360	3600 x 2880	3008 x 2400	2400 x 1920	1808 x 1440	1200 x 960	896 x 720	608 x 480
1:1	4000 x 4000	3840 x 3840	3360 x 3360	2880 x 2880	2400 x 2400	1920 x 1920	1440 x 1440	960 x 960	720 x 720	480 x 480
16:9	6000 x 3376	5760 x 3240	5120 x 2880	4480 x 2520	3840 x 2160	3200 x 1800	2560 x 1440	1920 x 1080	1280 x 720	960 x 536

Cross Screen, however, is an enigmatic name. It creates a "starburst" effect around light sources and other very bright points, like sparkling highlights on water. (Surely, **Star** would have been a better name?) There are multiple options within this item, including the number, angle and length of the star points.

› Color balance

Creates a copy with modified color balance. When this option is selected a preview screen appears and the Multi-selector can be used to move a cursor around a color grid. The effect is shown both in the preview and in the histograms alongside.

› Image overlay

Image overlay allows you to combine two existing photos into a new image. This can only be applied to originals in RAW format. Nikon claim that the results are better than combining the images in applications like Photoshop because Image overlay makes direct use of the raw data from the camera's sensor, but this is debatable; certainly, a large, calibrated computer screen gives you a much better preview of the result.

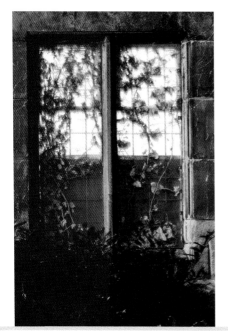

MONOCHROME   **«**
Comparison of Sepia (left) and Cyanotype Monochrome versions.

To create an overlaid image

1) In the Retouch menu, select **Image overlay** and press ⊛. The next screen has panels labelled **Image 1**, **Image 2**, and **Preview.** Initially, **Image 1** is highlighted. Press ⊛.

2) The camera displays thumbnails of RAW images on the memory card. Select the first image required for the overlay and press ⊛. Press ▶ to move to Image 2 and select the second image.

3) Use the **Gain** control below each image to determine its "weight" in the final overlay. The preview changes to show the effect.

4) Use ◀ and ▶ to move between Images 1 and 2 if further changes are required. You can press ⊛ to change the selected image.

5) Finally, press ▶ to reach the **Preview** panel. With Overlay highlighted, press ⚲ to preview the overlay. Return to the main screen by pressing ⚲⊞. To save the combined image, highlight **Save** and press ⊛.

› Resize

This option creates a small copy of the selected picture(s), suitable for immediate use with various external devices. Four possible sizes are available as follows in the table below.

Option	Size (pixels)	Possible uses
2.5M	1920 x 1280	Display on HD TV, larger computer monitor, new iPad.
1.1M	1280 x 856	Display on typical computer monitor, older iPad.
0.6M	960 x 640	Display on standard TV, iPhone 4/5.
0.3M	640 x 424	Display on majority of mobile devices.

› NEF (RAW) Processing

This menu creates JPEG copies from images originally shot as RAW files. It's no substitute for full RAW processing on computer (*see page 226*), but it does let you create quick copies for previewing or printing. Processing options are displayed in a column alongside a preview image (see the table below). When satisfied with the previewed image, scroll up to select **EXE**. Press ⊙ to create the JPEG copy. Pressing **MENU** exits without creating a copy.

Option	Description
Image quality	Choose Fine, Normal, or Basic (*see page 78*)
Image size	Choose Large, Medium, or Small (*see page 80*)
White balance	Choose a white balance setting; options are similar to those described on *page 83*
Exposure comp.	Adjust exposure (brightness) levels from +2 to −2
Set Picture Control	Choose any of the range of Nikon Picture Controls (*see page 99*) to be applied to the image
High ISO NR	Choose level of noise reduction where appropriate (*see page 113*)
Color space	Choose color space (*see page 84*)
D-Lighting	Choose D-Lighting level (High, Normal, Low, or Off) (*see page 127*)

› Quick retouch

Provides basic "quick fix" retouching, boosting saturation and contrast. D-Lighting is applied automatically to improve shadow detail. Use ◀ and ▶ to increase or reduce the strength of the effect, then press ⊙ to create the retouched copy.

› Straighten

It's best to get horizons level at the time of shooting, but it doesn't always work out. This option offers a fall-back, with correction up to 5° in 0.25° steps. Use ▶ to rotate clockwise, ◀ to rotate anticlockwise. Inevitably, this crops the image.

› Distortion control

Some lenses create noticeable curvature of straight lines (*see page 192*). This menu allows you to correct this in-camera. This inevitably crops the image slightly. **Auto** allows automatic compensation for the known characteristics of Type G and D Nikkor lenses (**Auto Distortion control**, in the Shooting menu, can apply this automatically to JPEG images).

If you have images taken with other lenses, you'll have to use **Manual** instead.

› Fisheye

Instead of correcting it, this exaggerates barrel distortion to give a fisheye lens effect. Use ▶ to increase the effect.

› Color Outline

This detects edges in the photograph and uses them to create a "line-drawing" effect. There are no options to alter the effect.

› Perspective control

Corrects the convergence of vertical lines in photos taken looking up, for example, at tall buildings. Grid lines help you assess the effect, and you control its strength with the Multi-selector. The process inevitably crops the image, so leave room around the subject when you shoot. For alternative approaches to perspective control, and an example, *see page 200*.

› Color Sketch

This creates a copy resembling a colored pencil drawing. Controls for Vividness and Outlines adjust the strength of the effect.

Also available as a Special Effect (*page 51*) when shooting.

COLOR SKETCH ⌄
A sample Color Sketch treatment of an image (Vividness and Outlines both set to maximum).

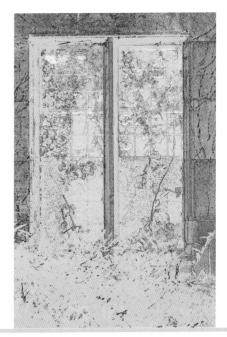

› Miniature effect

This option mimics the fad for shooting images with extremely localized depth of field, making real scenes look like miniature models. It usually works best with photos taken from a high viewpoint, which typically have clearer separation of foreground and background. A yellow rectangle shows the area which will remain in sharp focus. You can reposition and resize this using the Multi-selector. Press ⊕ to preview the results and press (OK) to save a retouched copy of the image.

Also available as a Special Effect (*page 52*) when shooting.

› Selective color

You can select up to three specific color(s) to be preserved in the retouched copy, while any other hues are transformed to monochrome.

1) Use the Multi-selector to place the cursor over an area of the desired color. Press *AE-L/AF-L* to choose that color.

2) To select another color, turn the Command Dial again to highlight another "swatch" and repeat steps 1 and 2.

3) To save the retouched copy, press (OK). Also available as a Special Effect (*page 52*) when shooting.

› Edit movie

This item merely allows you to trim the start and/or end of movie clips. Though far short of proper editing (*page 181*), it has its uses. To trim a movie clip:

1) Select a movie clip in full-frame playback (do not play the movie).

2) Press 🎬; select **Edit Movie** and press ▶.

3) Select **Choose start/end point** and press (OK). The screen shows the opening frame of the clip. Press *AE-L/AF-L* to jump between start and end points. Rotate the Command Dial to jump forward or back in 10-second steps.

4) Press (OK) to start playing the movie from the selected start/end point. Press ▼ to pause.

5) With the clip paused at the required point, press ▲ to set the start/end point. Select **Yes** and press (OK) to save the clip.

6) You can opt to **Save as new file** to create a trimmed copy while retaining the original. Alternatively, select **Overwrite existing file** to save the trimmed copy and delete the original (there's no going back).

7) Repeat if necessary to trim the other end of the clip.

3 » RECENT SETTINGS AND MY MENU

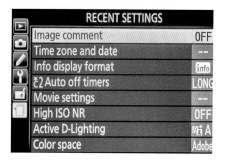

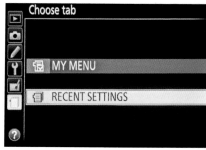

RECENT SETTINGS MENU ⌃

The Recent Settings menu automatically stores the most recent items that you have accessed from any of the other menus, providing a quick way to access controls that you have used recently. The list contains up to 20 items and so is likely to include any that you visit frequently.

Alternatively, you can activate My Menu. This lets you create a customized list of your "favorite" menu items. Again, it can store a maximum of 20 items.

Recent Settings is active by default and automatically records the items you've used. If you want to switch to My Menu, you'll need to activate it and then add items manually.

ACTIVATING MY MENU ⌃

To activate My Menu
1) In Recent Settings, select Choose tab and press ▶.

2) Select My Menu and press .

To add items to My Menu
1) Highlight **Add items** and press ▶.

2) A list of the other menus now appears. Select the appropriate menu and press ▶.

3) Select the desired menu item and press (OK).

4) A Choose position screen reappears with the newly added item at the top. Use ▲ / ▼ to reposition it in the list if desired. Press (OK) to confirm and save the list.

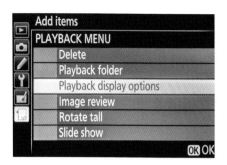

Add items
PLAYBACK MENU
  Delete
  Playback folder
  Playback display options
  Image review
  Rotate tall
  Slide show
                        OK OK

MY MENU   ⌃

To remove items from My Menu

1) Highlight Remove items and press ▶.

2) Highlight any item and press ▶ to select it for deletion. A check mark appears beside the item.

3) Select additional items in the same way.

4) Press ⊙. A confirmation dialog appears. To confirm the deletion(s) press ⊙ again. To exit without deleting anything, press **MENU**.

> ### *Tip*
>
> *A quicker way to delete a single item is to highlight it and press 🗑. To confirm deletion press 🗑 again.*

To rearrange items in My Menu

1) Highlight **Rank items** and press ▶.

2) Highlight any item and press ⊙.

3) Use ▲ or ▼ to move the item up or down—a yellow line shows where its new position will be. Press ⊙ to confirm the new position.

4) Repeat steps 2 and 3 to move further items. When finished, press **MENU** to exit.

There's a lot of nonsense talked about composition and above all about "rules" of composition. Composition—or framing, which is the word I prefer—is about what you can see and what you want to say about it. It's about what's in the picture and what's left out. It's about where you shoot from and the focal length you use. With all this going on, "rules", if they have any value at all, are a long way down the list and fretting about them just takes your mind off more important things.

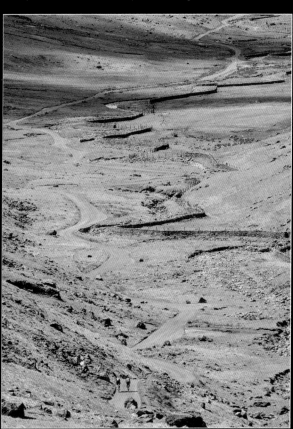

FILLING THE FRAME

The choices here were nothing to do with rules, but all about filling the frame. With my 70–200mm zoom lens at its longest setting, the zig-zag lines of the road—complemented by the walls and river—created a pattern which was quite striking even before the cyclists entered the shot. I took several shots as they travelled down the valley, but this first one, with them close to the bottom of the frame, was the strongest. It certainly helps that they both had red jerseys. Color is also an integral element in composition.

Settings
> ISO 400
> 1/1000 sec. at f/9
> 200mm lens

RULES DON'T RULE

Again, "rules" had nothing to contribute to the framing of this image. The light was changing fast and I had to work quickly and intuitively. The slightly choppy water of the lake was gray and didn't really reflect any of the vibrant color above, so I placed the shoreline low in the frame. The main elements were the rainbow, and the sunlight on the hill in the middle distance, and I tried to frame the shot so they felt balanced.

Settings
> ISO 1250
> 1/640 sec. at f/8
> 80mm lens

4 FLASH

Flash can be immensely useful, and the D5300 has great capabilities, but flash photography can also lead to confusion and frustration. Flash is not the answer to every low-light shot. Understanding its limitations helps us understand when to seek other options, as well as when and how we can use flash effectively.

› Principles

All flashguns are small; all flashguns are weak. These two statements are key to understanding flash photography. They are especially true for built-in units like that on the D5300 and most other DSLRs (the flash units on compact cameras are typically even smaller and weaker).

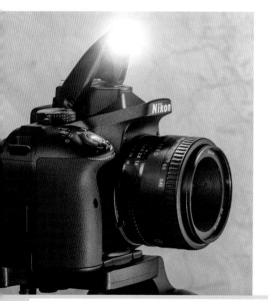

Because it's small, the flash produces very hard light. It's similar to direct sunlight, but even the strongest sunlight is slightly softened by scattering and reflection; we can use the same principles to soften the flash, too.

The weakness of flash is even more fundamental. All flashguns have a limited range, and on-camera flash is more limited than most accessory flashguns.

Built-in flash units raise a third issue, too, namely their fixed position close to the lens, which makes the light one-dimensional—and the same for every shot, which becomes boring. See Operating the built-in flash on *page 140*.

» FILL-IN FLASH

A key application for flash is for "fill-in" light, giving a lift to dark shadows like those cast by direct sunlight. This is why pros regularly use flash in bright sunlight (exactly when most people would think it unnecessary).

Fill-in flash doesn't need to illuminate the shadows fully, only to lighten them a little. This means the flash can be used at a smaller aperture, or greater distance, than when it's the main light (averaging around 2 Ev smaller, or four times the distance).

FILL-IN FLASH ⩔
The background exposure is the same for both shots, and really the difference made by the flash is only obvious when you look at the faces—but faces matter. *16mm, 1/200 sec., f/8, ISO 200.*

› i-TTL balanced fill-flash for DSLR

Nikon's i-TTL balanced fill-flash helps achieve natural-looking results when using fill-in flash. It comes into play automatically provided (a) matrix or center-weighted metering is selected and (b) a CPU-equipped lens is attached: most of the time, in other words.

The flash (built-in or compatible flashgun) emits a series of virtually invisible pre-flashes immediately before exposure. Light reflected from these pre-flashes is detected by the metering sensor and analyzed, together with the ambient light. If Type D or G lenses are used, distance information is also incorporated.

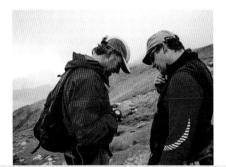
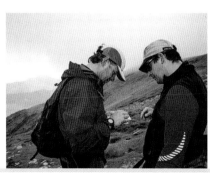

› Standard i-TTL flash for DSLR

If spot metering is selected, this mode is activated instead (it can also be selected directly on some accessory flashguns). The camera controls flash output to light the subject correctly, but makes no attempt to balance it with background illumination. This mode is more appropriate when flash is the main light source, rather than providing fill light.

I-TTL BALANCED FILL-FLASH ⩔
i-TTL balanced fill-flash for DSLR gives a very natural result; it's not overly obvious that flash has been used at all, but without it the interior of the cave would be virtually black. *18mm, 1/200 sec., f/14, ISO 200.*

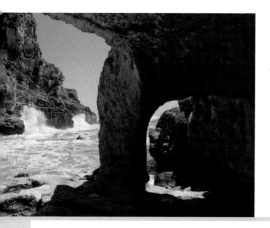

› Operating the built-in flash

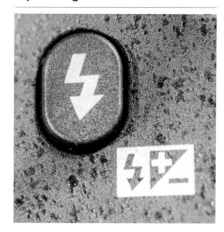

THE ⚡ BUTTON ⩘

The D5300's built-in flash, like all such units, is small, low-powered, and fixed in position close to the lens axis. Together, these factors mean it has a limited range, and produces a flat and harsh light which is unpleasant for portraits and most other subjects. It's certainly better than nothing at times, but its real value is for fill-in light.

In 🅰 Auto, and many of the Scene modes, the flash activates when the camera deems it necessary (**Auto flash**), though it can always be turned off. In ⚡ Auto (flash off), and certain Scene modes, the built-in flash is not available. In P, S, A, or M modes and 🍴 Food, the flash is always available but you must activate it manually as follows.

› Activating the built-in flash

1) Select a metering method (*see page 64*). Matrix metering is advised for fill-in flash. Spot metering is appropriate when flash is the main light.

2) Press ⚡ and the flash will pop up and begin charging. When it is charged the ready indicator ⚡ is displayed in the Viewfinder.

3) Choose a flash mode from the Active Information Display. Highlight the current flash mode and press ⊙K. Select the desired flash mode and press ⊙K again. (*See page 142* for a detailed explanation of flash modes.)

4) Take the photo(s) in the normal way.

5) When finished, lower the built-in flash, pressing gently down until it clicks into place.

> ### *Tip*
>
> *The built-in flash is recommended for use with CPU lenses between 18mm and 300mm focal length. Some lenses may block part of the flash output at close range; removing the lens hood often helps. The* Nikon Reference Manual *details limitations of use with certain lenses.*

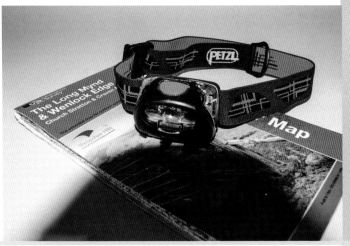

SHADOW »
Even with the lens hood removed, the built-in flash can throw a very obvious shadow, especially on close-up subjects.

» FLASH EXPOSURE

Whether the shutter speed is 1/200 sec. or 20 sec., the flash normally fires just once and therefore delivers the same amount of light to the subject. In the absence of other light, the subject would look the same whatever the shutter speed. Shutter speed becomes relevant when there is other light around, which we call ambient light. Slower shutter speeds give more chance for the ambient light to register.

Aperture, however, is relevant to both flash exposure and ambient exposure. The camera's flash metering takes this into account but it is useful to understand this distinction for a clearer sense of what's going on, especially with slow-sync shots.

The combinations of shutter speed and aperture that are available when using flash depend on the exposure mode in use.

Exposure mode	Shutter speed	Aperture
P	Set by camera. The normal range is between 1/200 and 1/60 sec., but in certain flash modes all settings up to 30 sec. are available.	Set by camera
S	Selected by user. All settings between 1/200 sec. and 30 sec. are available. If user sets a faster shutter speed, the D5300 will fire at 1/200 sec. while the flash is active.	Set by camera
A	Set by camera. The normal range is between 1/200 and 1/60 sec., but in certain flash modes all settings up to 30 sec. are available.	Set by camera
M	Selected by user. All settings between 1/200 sec. and 30 sec. are available. If user sets a faster shutter speed, the D5300 will fire at 1/200 sec. while the flash is active.	Set by camera
AUTO 📷 🌷 🌃 🏃 🐕 🍴 🌅 🧸	Set by camera, between 1/200 and 1/60 sec.	Set by camera
🤰	Set by camera, between 1/200 and 1/60 sec. (1/30 sec. when Vibration Reduction is in use).	Set by camera
🏔	Set by camera, between 1/200 and 1 sec.	Set by camera

› Flash range

The range of any flash depends on its power, ISO sensitivity setting and the aperture set. The table below details the approximate range of the built-in flash for selected distances, apertures, and ISO settings. The table is based on Nikon's own figures, confirmed by practical tests. There's no need to memorize these figures, but it does help to have a sense of the limited range that always applies when using flash. A quick test shot will tell you if any given subject is within range.

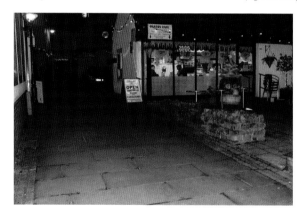

FLASH RANGE «
Even at ISO 1600, the limited range of the built-in flash is obvious. It doesn't really even reach as far as the café (but note that it does reflect off a car number plate further back).

| ISO equivalent setting | | | | | | Range | |
100	200	400	800	1600	3200	(feet and inches)	(meters)
1.4	2	2.8	4	5.6	8	3ft 3in.–27ft 11in.	1.0–8.5
2	2.8	4	5.6	8	11	2ft 4in.–20ft	0.7–6.1
2.8	4	5.6	8	11	16	2ft–13ft 9 in.	0.6–4.2
4	5.6	8	11	16	22	2ft–9ft 10 in.	0.6–3.0
5.6	8	11	16	22	32	2f–6ft 11 in.	0.6–2.1
8	11	16	22	32		2ft–4ft 11 in.	0.6–1.5
11	16	22	32			2ft–3ft 7 in.	0.6–1.1
16	22	32				2ft–2ft 4 in.	0.6–0.7

› Guide Numbers

The Guide Number (GN) is a measure of the power of a flash. In the past, photographers used GNs constantly to calculate flash exposures and working range. With modern flash metering, like Nikon's i-TTL system (see below), such computations are rarely needed. However, the GN does help us to compare different flashguns. For instance, the GN for the built-in flash is 12 (meters, ISO 100); for the Nikon SB-910 it is 34, indicating almost three times the power. This allows shooting at three times the distance, at a lower ISO, or with a smaller aperture.

Tip

GNs are specified in feet and/or meters and usually for an ISO rating of 100. When comparing different units, be sure that both GNs are stated in the same terms.

› Flash synchronization and flash modes

Flash, as the name implies, is virtually instantaneous, lasting just a few milliseconds. If the flash is to cover the whole image frame it must be fired when the shutter is fully open, but at faster shutter speeds DSLRs like the D5300 do not

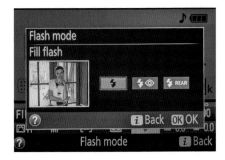

FLASH MODE SETTING IN THE ACTIVE INFORMATION DISPLAY

in fact expose the whole frame at once. In the case of the D5300, the fastest shutter speed which can be used with flash is 1/200 sec. This is therefore known as the sync (for synchronization) speed.

Flash modes are distinguished by how they regulate synchronization and shutter speed. Choose a flash mode by pressing ⚡ and rotating the Command Dial, or using the Active Information Display.

Standard flash mode (front-curtain sync)

This is the default flash mode in most exposure modes. However, the flash mode item in the Active Information Display labels it "Fill-flash" when using P, S, A, and M exposure modes and "Auto flash" in other modes.

In standard flash operation, the flash fires as soon as the shutter is fully open, i.e. as soon as possible after the shutter-release button is pressed. This gives a fast response and the best chance of capturing the subject as you see it. However, it can create odd-looking results when dealing with moving subjects—for these, rear-curtain sync (see below) may be more suitable.

In P and A exposure modes, the camera will set a shutter speed in the range 1/60–1/200 sec. In S and M exposure modes, you can set any shutter speed down to 30 sec., which means that standard flash also encompasses Slow sync (see below).

Slow sync

This mode allows longer shutter speeds (right up to 30 sec.) to be used in P and A exposure modes, so that backgrounds can be captured even in low ambient light. Movement of the subject or camera (or even both) can result in a partly blurred image created by the ambient light, combined with a sharp image where the subject is lit by the flash. This may sometimes be unwelcome, but can also be used for creative effect.

This mode is also available, in a limited form (longest exposure 1 sec.), with 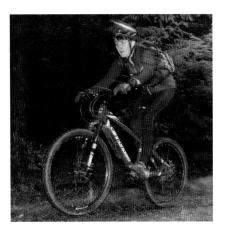 Night portrait mode—here it's labelled **Auto slow sync.** You can't select Slow sync in S and M exposure modes, but it isn't necessary, as longer shutter speeds are available anyway.

Rear-curtain sync

Rear-curtain sync triggers the flash not at the first available moment (as front-curtain

SLOW SYNC ⌃
Slow sync combines a flash image with a motion-blurred image from the ambient light, but front-curtain sync makes the blurred elements run ahead of the flash image, not behind it.

REAR-CURTAIN SYNC ⌄
Rear-curtain sync means that the motion-blurred elements of the image appear behind the sharp image created by the flash.

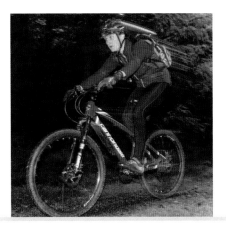

sync does), but at the last possible instant. This makes sense when photographing moving subjects because any image of the subject created by the ambient light then appears behind the sharp flash image, which looks more natural than having it appear to extend ahead of the direction of movement. Rear-curtain sync can only be selected when using P, S, A, and M exposure modes. In P and A modes it also allows slow shutter speeds (below 1/60 sec.) to be used, and is then called **slow rear-curtain sync.**

When using longer exposure times, shooting with rear-curtain sync can be tricky, as you need to predict where your subject will be at the end of the exposure, rather than immediately after pressing the shutter-release button. It is often best suited to working with cooperative subjects—or naturally repeating action, like races over numerous laps of a circuit—so you can fine-tune your timing after reviewing images on the monitor.

Red-eye reduction

On-camera flash often creates "red-eye", caused by light reflecting off the subject's retina. Red-eye reduction works by shining a light (the AF-assist illuminator) at the subject just before the exposure, causing their pupils to contract. This creates a delay, which kills spontaneity and may mean missing the shot entirely. Generally, it's better to remove red-eye in post-

processing or with **Red-eye correction** in the Retouch menu (*see page 128*). Alternatively, use a separate flash, or up the ISO rating and avoid flash altogether.

Unfortunately, red-eye reduction is on by default in 🎉 Party/indoor, but can be changed in the Active Information Display.

Red-eye reduction with slow sync

This combines the two modes named, allowing backgrounds to register. This mode is only available when using P and A exposure modes and, in a more limited form, with 🌙 Night portrait.

› Flash compensation

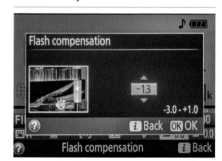

SETTING FLASH COMPENSATION ⌃
IN THE ACTIVE INFORMATION DISPLAY

Although the D5300's flash metering is extremely sophisticated, it's not 100% infallible. You may also want to adjust flash output for creative effect. Image review helps you assess the effect of the flash, allowing compensation to be applied with confidence to further shots.

Flash compensation is only available in P, S, A, and M modes and is activated via the Active Information Display. Alternatively, press ⚡ and ± and rotate the Command Dial. This requires some dexterity, but can be quicker.

Compensation can be set from −3 Ev to +1 Ev in increments of ⅓ Ev. Positive compensation will brighten areas lit by the flash, but have no effect on areas lit by other light sources (ambient light). However, if the subject is already at the limit of the flash range, positive compensation can't make it any brighter. Negative compensation reduces the brightness of flash-lit areas, again while leaving other areas unaffected.

After use, reset flash compensation to zero. Otherwise the camera will retain the setting next time you use flash.

› Manual flash

By using the **Manual** option in Custom setting e1, **Flash cntrl for built-in flash**, you can control flash output even more precisely, from full power to as low as 1/32 power.

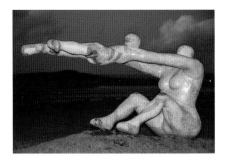
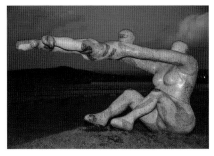
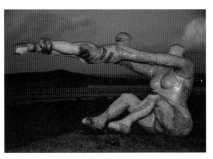

MANUAL FLASH ADJUSTMENT ⌃
The background exposure remains the same, but the flash level on the sculpture varies, with compensation set to (from top) +1, 0, and −1, respectively. *65mm, 1/5 sec., f/5.6, ISO 400.*

» USING OPTIONAL SPEEDLIGHTS

If you're serious about portrait or close-up photography, in particular, you'll soon find the built-in flash inadequate. Accessory flashguns, which Nikon calls Speedlights, enormously extend the power and flexibility of flash with the D5300. Nikon Speedlights integrate fully with Nikon's Creative Lighting System for outstanding results using flash. There are currently four models, all highly sophisticated units mainly aimed at professional and advanced users, and priced accordingly. The flagship SB-910 is particularly impressive—but costs more than many Nikkor lenses.

Independent makers such as Sigma offer alternatives, some of them also compatible with Nikon's i-TTL flash control. However, such "dedicated" units are also hardly cheap.

Many possibilities can be explored with much cheaper flashguns. For instance, any flashgun, however basic, that allows manual triggering with a "test" button can be used for the "painting with light" technique outlined below.

You may have an old flashgun at the back of a cupboard, and it's always worth checking the bargain bin at the local camera shop.

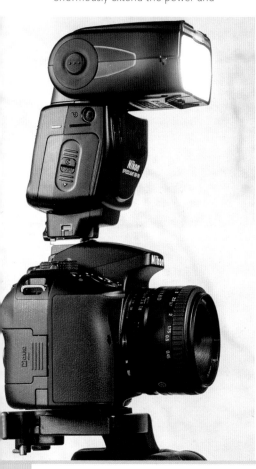

> ### *Tip*
>
> *Speedlights are greedy for battery power. It is always wise to carry at least one set of spares.*

D5300 AND SPEEDLIGHT SB-700 **«**

Mounting an external Speedlight

1) Check that the camera and the Speedlight are both switched off, and that the pop-up flash is down. Remove the hotshoe cover.

2) Slide the foot of the Speedlight into the camera's hotshoe. If it does not slide easily, check whether the mounting lock on the Speedlight is in the locked position.

3) Rotate the lock lever at the base of the Speedlight to secure it in position.

4) Switch on both the camera and the Speedlight.

Tip

Most surfaces will absorb some of the light, and in any case the light has to travel further to reach the subject; i-TTL metering will automatically adjust for this, but the effective range is reduced. Bounce flash works better in domestic interiors with fairly low ceilings (especially if they are white or light in color) than in larger spaces. Alternatively, you can use a reflector.

› Bounce flash and off-camera flash

The fixed position of the built-in flash throws odd shadows on nearby subjects and makes portraits ugly. A hotshoe-mounted Speedlight will improve things slightly, but you can make a much bigger difference by either:

1) Bouncing the flash light off a ceiling, wall or reflector.

2) Taking the Speedlight off the camera.

Bounce flash

Bouncing the flash light off a suitable surface both spreads the light, softening hard-edged shadows, and changes its direction, eliminating the flatness of direct on-camera flash.

Nikon's SB-910 and SB-700 Speedlights have heads which can be tilted and swivelled through a wide range, allowing light to be bounced off walls, ceilings, and other surfaces. The SB-400 has a more limited tilt capability, allowing light to be bounced off the ceiling or a reflector.

› Off-camera flash

Taking the flash off the camera gives you
complete control over the direction of the
light. The flash can be fired using a flash
cord. Nikon's dedicated cords preserve
i-TTL metering (*see page 139*).

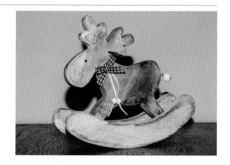

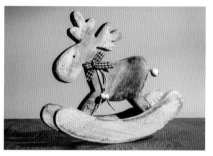

DIRECTIONAL FLASH »
The first shot (top) was taken using the built-in
flash, making this three-dimensional
arrangement look distinctly flat. The center shot
uses indirect flash from the right. The image
below uses flash bounced off a ceiling, giving
softer, more even light, but retaining a 3D
quality. Notice there's also a color shift because
the bounce surface is not a neutral reflector.
62mm, f/11, ISO 100.

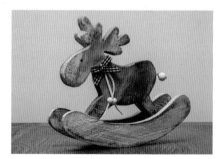

› Painting with light

You can try this with any flashgun, even the cheapest, that can be triggered manually. By firing multiple flashes at the subject from different directions, you build up overall coverage of light without losing the sparkle that directional light gives. It requires trial and error, but that's part of the fun. The basic steps are:

1) Set up so that neither camera nor subject can move during the exposure.

2) Use Manual mode. Set a long shutter speed such as 20 or 30 seconds, or even B. Set a small aperture such as f/16 (this may need trial and error). Focus on the subject then turn the focus selector to M so the camera doesn't try to refocus.

3) Turn out the lights. It helps to have just enough background light to see what you are doing, but no more.

4) Trip the shutter and then fire the flash at the subject from different directions (without aiming directly into the lens).

5) Review the result and start again! For example, if results are too bright, use fewer flashes, a lower ISO, a smaller aperture, hold the flash further away, or a combination. If the flash has a variable power setting this could be turned down.

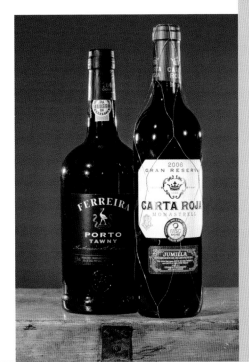

PAINTING WITH LIGHT »
This image was created with five bursts of flash: two from the front left, to illuminate the darkest areas, and one each from the back left, back right and front right. *7mm, 15 sec., f/16, ISO 800.*

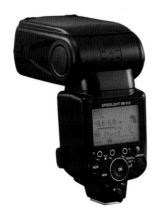

The table below summarizes key features ⌄
of current Nikon Speedlights.

› Wireless flash

Nikon's Creative Lighting System includes the ability to regulate the light from multiple Speedlights through a wireless system. The built-in flash units on professional DSLRs like the D800 can be used as the "commander" for a wireless setup, as can the SB-910 and SB-700 Speedlights. There's also a standalone commander, the SU-800. The D5300 can operate within such a system but must be physically connected to a commander unit. There are alternative wireless systems too, like Pocket Wizard and Phottix Odin.

	SB-910	SB-700	SB-400	SB-R200
Flash coverage (lens focal length range, mm)	17–200	24–120		
Guide Number (ISO 100, meters)	34	28	21	
Tilt/swivel	Yes	Tilt only	No	
Dimensions (width x height x depth, mm)	78.5 x 145 x 113	71 x 126 x 104.5	66 x 56.5 x 80	80 x 75 x 55
Weight (without batteries)	420g	360g	127g	120g
Use as commander?	Yes	Yes	No	No (cannot be camera hotshoe, only as a slave within Creative Lighting System)

WIRELESS FLASH ⌄

A Nikon Speedlight SB-700 was placed on a tripod almost in line with the barrier. I used the Phottix Odin radio system to control the flash, but very similar results are possible using Nikon's own SU-800 or indeed using a sync lead, though a wireless system gives the photographer more freedom to move around. The flash is nicely balanced with the ambient lighting, but it does make the image of the rider both brighter and sharper.
31mm, 1/200 sec., f/9, ISO 200.

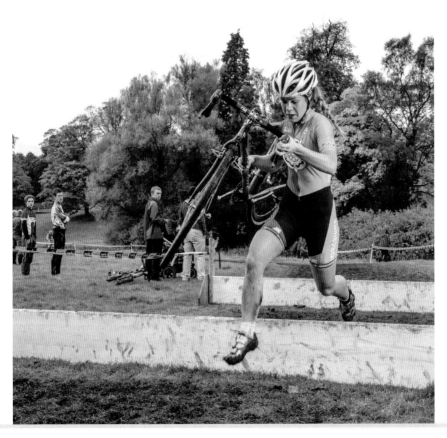

» FLASH ACCESSORIES

To add even more flexibility and control of lighting effects, a wide variety of flash accessories is available. Nikon has an extensive range, and some third-party suppliers offer even more, but when time is short or money is tight substitutes can often be improvized.

Battery packs

Nikon produces add-on power packs for some of its Speedlights to speed up recycling and extend battery life.

Color filters

Flash filters can be used to create striking color effects, or to match the color of the flash to that of the background lighting. Nikon produces various filters to fit its Speedlight range.

Flash cords

Because the D5300's built-in flash can't act as a wireless commander, you can only maintain full metering and control of an external Speedlight if it's physically connected to the camera, either in the hotshoe or using a flash cord (also known as a sync lead). Dedicated cords like Nikon's SC-28 allow full communication between camera and Speedlight, retaining i-TTL flash control. The SC-28 extends up to 8 feet or 2.5 meters.

Flash diffusers

Flash diffusers are a simple, economical way to spread and soften the hard light from a flashgun. They may slide over the flash head or be attached by low-tech means like elastic bands or Velcro. Sto-Fen make Omni-Bounce diffusers to fit most flashguns. Even a white handkerchief can be used at a pinch (but beware, flash units can get hot). Diffusers reduce the light reaching the subject—the D5300's metering system will allow for this, but the effective range will be shorter.

A D5300 AND A HONL "SOFTBOX" ❱❱

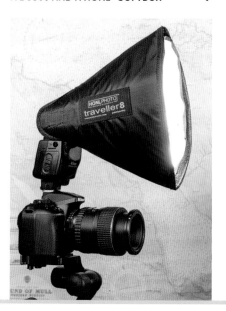

A step beyond a simple diffuser is the portable "softbox" which can attach to a Speedlight to create a wider spread of light.

Flash extenders

A flash extender slips over the flash head, using mirrors or a lens to create a tighter beam and extend the effective range of the flash. Again, the D5300's metering system will automatically accommodate the use of an extender. Nikon do not make flash extenders, so a third-party option will be required.

Flash brackets

The ability to take the flash off the camera, and therefore change the angle at which the light hits the subject, is invaluable in controlling the quality of light. Nikon's Speedlights can be mounted on a tripod or stand on any flat surface using the AS-19 stand, but for a quick, portable solution many photographers prefer a light, flexible arm or bracket which attaches to the camera and supports the Speedlight. Novoflex produces a range of such products.

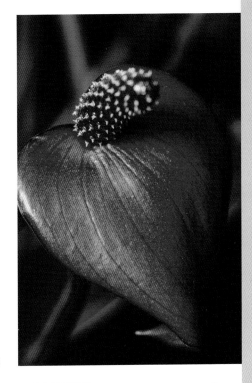

FLASH DIFFUSER ⌃
This shot was taken using the HONL flash diffuser on a Speedlight SB-700 with a remote cord, fired from the left of the subject. *100mm macro, 1/60 sec., f/16, ISO 100.*

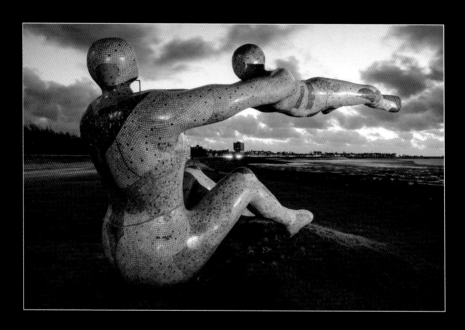

LIGHT FANTASTIC

Another view of the sculpture seen on *page 147*. The reverse angle means the sky is brighter and also brings streetlights and traffic into the reckoning. A four-second exposure stretched the lights of moving cars into abstract trails. The flash was off-camera on the right. It took a couple of attempts before I was satisfied with both the position of the flash and its brightness level.

Settings
> ISO 400
> 4 sec. at f/16
> 18mm lens

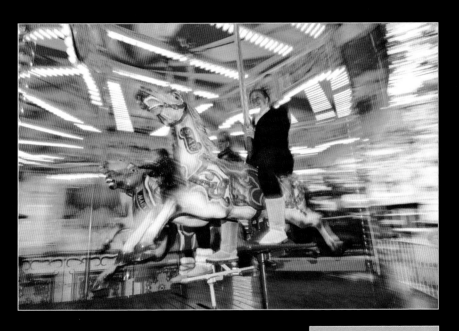

NIGHT RIDER

For this shot I used a wide-angle lens and a panning technique, combined with flash to give a sharp image of the nearest horse and rider. After taking a couple of test shots, I reduced the strength of the flash slightly to balance it with the available ambient light.

Settings
> ISO 800
> 1/15 sec. at f/11
> 14mm lens

5 CLOSE-UP

For close-up photography the 35mm SLR and digital successors like the D5300 have long reigned supreme. Reflex viewing, once essential in close-up work, is now supplemented by Live View. Also, the D5300 is part of the legendary Nikon system of lenses and accessories, which offers many additional options for close-up photography.

Because depth of field is so slim, focusing becomes critical. Merely focusing on "the subject" is no longer good enough and you must decide which part of the subject—for instance, an insect's eye,

UP CLOSE ⌄

Close-up subjects are everywhere, and close-up photography really makes us look more attentively. *100mm macro, 1/50 sec., f/11, ISO 200, tripod.*

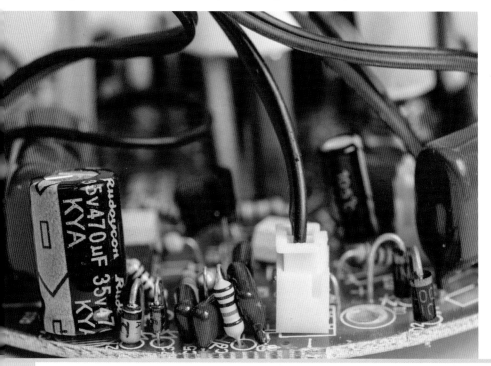

the stamen of a flower—should be the point of sharp focus. With its 39 AF points, the D5300 is capable of focusing accurately within much of the frame, but this is also where Live View really shines. In ⊞ Wide-area AF or ⊞ Normal area AF (*see page 92*), the focus point can be set anywhere in the frame. Live View, with its ability to zoom in, also makes manual focusing ultra-precise—and it's impeccably accurate. For years I was a "Live View

Luddite" but now it's my first choice for macro photography, especially with static subjects.

POINT OF FOCUS ⌄
In extreme close-up shooting, depth of field is minimal even at smaller apertures. This makes accurate focusing essential—and this begins with precise placement of the focus point. *100mm macro, 1/400 sec., f/11, ISO 200.*

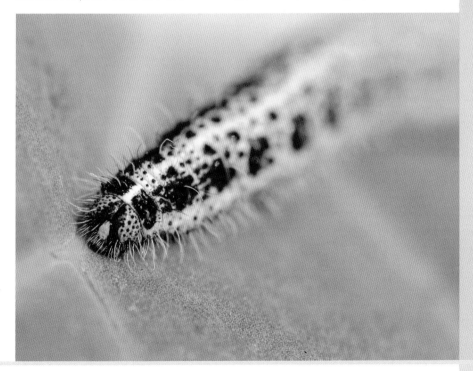

5 » MACRO PHOTOGRAPHY

There's no exact definition of "close-up", but "macro" should be used more precisely. Macro photography really means photography of objects at life-size or larger, implying a reproduction ratio (see below) of at least 1:1. Many zoom lenses are branded "macro" when their reproduction ratio is around 1:4, or 1:2 at best. This still allows much fascinating close-up photography, but it isn't "proper" macro.

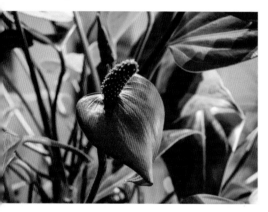

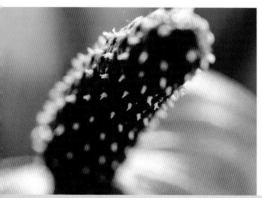

› Reproduction ratio

The reproduction ratio (or image magnification) is the ratio between the actual size of the subject and the size of its image on the D5300's imaging sensor, which measures 0.9in. x 0.6in. or 23.5mm x 15.6mm. An object of the same dimensions (smaller than an SD memory card) captured at 1:1 would exactly fill the image frame. When the image is printed, or displayed on a computer screen, it may appear many times larger, but that's another story.

A 1:4 reproduction ratio means that the smallest subject that would give you a frame-filling shot is one that's four times as long or wide as the sensor. With DX-format cameras like the D5300 this is about 3.7in. x 2.5in. or 94mm x 62mm— a fraction larger than a credit card.

MACRO-COSM 〈〈
The first shot (top left) has a reproduction ratio of approximately 1:4; this is about as good as you'll get with most "normal" lenses. The second (left), taken with a macro lens at the closest possible distance, gives approximately life size (1:1) reproduction. *70mm (top left) and 100mm (left) macro, 1 sec., f/11, ISO 800.*

› Working distance

Working distance is the distance required to obtain the desired reproduction ratio with any given lens. It is directly related to the focal length of the lens: with a 200mm macro lens the working distance for 1:1 reproduction is double what it is with a 100mm (roughly, 19.6in. or 50cm rather than 9.8in. or 25cm). The extra distance can be a big help when photographing living subjects, especially mobile ones. It can also be helpful with delicate subjects, living or not, which might be damaged by accidental contact.

Tip

Working distance and the minimum focus distance of a lens are normally measured from the subject to the focal plane, or the position of the sensor. A 9.8in. or 25cm working distance therefore means the subject, or the bit of the subject you're focusing on, can be less than 3.9in. or 10cm from the front of the lens. Other paraphernalia like lens hoods or ring-flash can reduce this gap even more.

» MACRO LIGHTING

Of course, many fine close-up and macro shots can be taken using available light. However, you'll often find that your own shadow, or the camera's, can intrude. Many subjects (like the interiors of flowers) can create their own shadows too. For these and other reasons, you'll soon start to want more controlled lighting. This usually means flash, but regular Speedlights are not designed for ultra-close work. If mounted on the hotshoe, short working distances mean that the lens may throw a shadow onto the subject. This is even worse with the built-in flash, which is essentially useless for real close-up photography.

› Improvization

Dedicated macro-flash units aren't cheap, and may be unjustifiable when you only shoot macro occasionally. Fortunately, you can do lots with a standard flashgun, plus a flash cord. With basic units, you'll lose the advanced flash control, but it only takes a few test shots to establish settings that you can use repeatedly (keep notes of what you try). Also essential is a small reflector, like a piece of white card—place it close to the subject for maximum benefit. This setup is cheap, flexible, and can deliver very polished results. Also, a flash diffuser, like a HONL, can give excellent results.

5

› Macro flash

Specialist macro flash usually takes the
form of either ring-flash or twin flash.
Because operating distances are short,
units do not need high power and can
be relatively light and compact.

Ring-flash units encircle the lens, giving
even illumination even on ultra-close
subjects (they're also preferred by some
portrait photographers). Nikon no longer
makes a ring-flash, but alternatives come
from Sigma and Nissin.

Nikon itself favors a twin-flash approach
with its Speedlight Commander Kit R1C1
and Speedlight Remote Kit R1. Both use
two Speedlight SB-R200 flashguns,
mounting either side of the lens. The
R1C1 uses a Wireless Speedlight
Commander SU-800 unit which fits into
the camera's hotshoe, while the R1 needs
a separate Speedlight to act as
commander. These kits are expensive
but give very flexible and precisely
controllable light on macro subjects.

› LED light

An alternative is to use LED lights, like the
Sunpak LED Macro Ring Light. Its
continuous output allows you to preview
the image in a way not possible with flash.
Its low power limits it to very close, and
usually static, subjects. But, then again,
it is cheap.

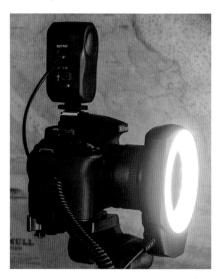

**D5300 AND SUNPAK LED MACRO
RING LIGHT** ≫

» EQUIPMENT FOR MACRO PHOTOGRAPHY

› Close-up attachment lenses

Close-up attachment lenses are simple magnifying lenses that screw into the filter thread of the lens. They are light, convenient, and inexpensive, and fully compatible with the camera's exposure and focusing systems. For best results, it's recommended to use them with prime lenses (*see page 187*).

Nikon produces six close-up attachment lenses, see the table below.

› Extension tubes

Extension tubes are another simple, relatively inexpensive, way of extending the close-focusing capabilities of a lens. An extension tube is essentially a simple tube fitting between the lens and the camera. This decreases the minimum focusing distance and thereby increases the magnification factor. Again they are light, compact and easy to carry and attach.

The Nikon system includes four Extension tubes, PK-11A, PK-12, PK-13,

and PN-11, which extend the lens by 8mm, 14mm, 27.5mm, and 52.5mm respectively. The PK-11 incorporates a tripod mount. The basic design of these tubes has not changed for many years, which means that many of the camera's functions are not available. In particular, there's no autofocus. Used on the D5300, you may be restricted to Manual (M) mode and exposure determination will be by trial and error—but that's what the histogram's for.

Kenko also produces compatible extension tubes, which do support matrix metering, although they still do not permit autofocus on the D5300. They're also far more reasonably priced than Nikon's own offerings.

Warning!

Some recent lenses are not compatible with accessories such as extension rings, bellows (see next page), and teleconverters (*see pages 164, 201*). Check the lens manual.

Product number	Attaches to filter thread	Recommended for use with
0, 1	52mm	Standard lenses
3T, 4T	52mm	Short telephoto lenses
5T, 6T	62mm	Telephoto lenses

› Bellows

Like extension tubes, bellows extend the spacing between the lens and the camera body, but they are not restricted to a few set lengths. Again, there's no extra glass to impair optical quality. However, bellows are expensive, heavy, and take time to set up. They are usually employed in a studio or other controlled setting.

Nikon's PB-6 bellows offers extensions from 48mm to 208mm, giving a maximum reproduction ratio of about 11:1. Focusing and exposure are manual only.

› Reversing rings

Also known as reverse adaptors or inversion rings, these allow lenses to be mounted in reverse; the adaptor screws into the filter thread. This allows much closer focusing than when the lens is used normally. They are ideally used with a prime lens, such as the classic 50mm f/1.8—Nikon's inversion ring BR-2A fits a 52mm filter thread.

› Light reduction

Because accessories like extension tubes and bellows increase the effective physical length of the lens, they also increase the effective focal length. However, the physical size of the aperture does not change. The result is to make the lens "slower"; that is, a lens with a maximum aperture of f/2.8 behaves like an f/4 or f/5.6 lens. This makes the Viewfinder image dimmer than normal, and affects the exposure required; the camera's metering will accommodate this, but you may need a longer shutter speed or more light. Reversing rings do not have this effect.

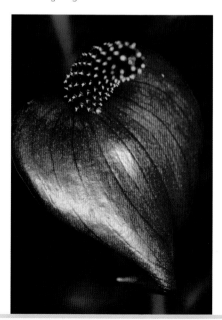

MACRO LIGHTING EQUIPMENT »
This shot was taken with the Sunpak Ring Light. It gives even, almost shadowless illumination on the subject, but there is a bit of glare. *100mm macro, 1.6 sec., f/16, ISO 100, tripod.*

» MACRO LENSES

True macro lenses achieve reproduction ratios of 1:1 or better and are optically optimized for close-up work, though normally very capable for general photography too. This is certainly true of Nikon's Micro Nikkor lenses, of which there are currently five.

The most recent addition to the range is the **40mm f/2.8G AF-S DX Micro Nikkor**; like the 85mm model (below) it's specifically designed for DX format cameras like the D5300. It's also Nikon's lightest, and least expensive, macro lens. Be aware, however that its working distance at 1:1 reproduction ratio is just 6.3in. or 16cm, leaving very little room between the subject and the front of the lens.

The **60mm f/2.8G ED AF-S Micro Nikkor** is an upgrade to the previous 60mm f/2.8D. Advances include ED glass for superior optical quality and Silent Wave Motor for ultra-quiet autofocus.

The **85mm f/3.5G ED VR AF-S DX Micro Nikkor** also achieves 1:1 reproduction and has VRII, internal focusing, and ED glass.

The **105mm f/2.8G AF-S VR Micro Nikkor** also features internal focusing, ED glass and Silent Wave Motor; it was also the world's first macro lens with VR (Vibration Reduction).

Though rather more venerable, the **200mm f/4D ED-IF AF Micro Nikkor** is particularly suitable for shooting the animal kingdom, as its longer working distance reduces the risk of disturbing your subject. This lens lacks a built-in motor and so can't autofocus with the D5300; this can be an issue when shooting lively animals, but it's not a problem when shooting static subjects.

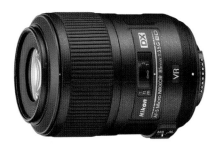

40MM F/2.8G AF-S DX MICRO NIKKOR ☆   **85MM F/3.5G ED VR AF-S DX MICRO NIKKOR** ☆

As the slightest camera shake is magnified at high reproduction ratios, VR (Vibration Reduction) technology is extremely welcome, allowing you to employ shutter speeds up to four stops slower than otherwise possible. However, it can't compensate for movement of the subject. Remember, too, that at close range the slightest change in subject–camera distance can completely ruin the focus, so a tripod is still invaluable.

GOOD VIBRATIONS

Vibration Reduction (VR) can be a big help in securing sharp images when shooting handheld—but camera–subject distance is still critical. *50mm macro, 1/125sec., f/8, ISO 400.*

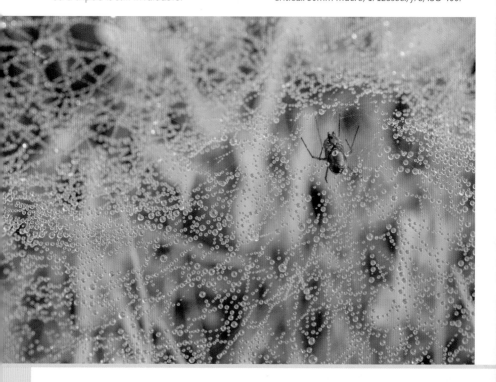

» NEW WAYS OF SEEING

Most photography is about capturing what you can see with the naked eye. Close-up photography goes beyond this into a whole new world, or at least a new way of seeing the world.

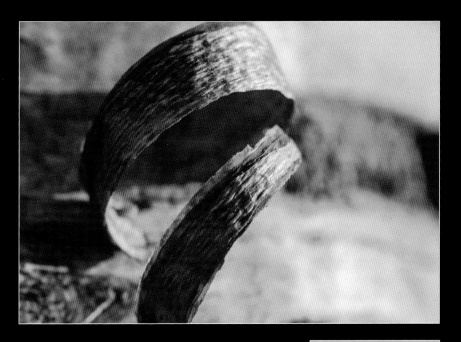

TREE OF LIGHT
A simple detail of a birch tree, which I'd walked past several times, but only noticed when it was highlighted by the evening sun.

Settings
> ISO 200
> 1/30 sec. at f/16
> 100mm macro lens

6 MOVIES

Nikon pioneered movies on DSLRs, launching the D90 in August 2008. For many, the true purpose of the SLR is to shoot stills and its ergonomics are still best for this, but the addition of video is no mere sideshow. Dedicated movie makers have embraced DSLRs for their distinctive image quality, while photojournalists welcome the ability to shoot high-quality stills and video on the same camera. However, still photography and movies are very different media, requiring quite different approaches for the best results.

Movie size and quality

The D5300 can shoot movies in Full HD (High Definition) quality with a frame size of 1920 x 1080 pixels. It can also record 1280 x 720-pixel ("720p") and 640 x 424-pixel footage. Shooting at the maximum frame size is by no means always essential. For example, 720p is the standard on Vimeo.com, a prime site for quality video online, and will look excellent on most computer screens. However, the latest iPads have a 2048 x 1536 display, boasting more pixels than Full HD.

Smaller size settings allow you to record more video on the same memory card, and consume less disk space on your computer. However, it must be said, footage shot in Full HD may be more "future-proof".

Advantages

DSLRs in general, and the D5300 in particular, have several real advantages over standard camcorders. One is the ability to achieve very shallow depth of field (see page 60); movie-makers have embraced this "DSLR look". This is a direct consequence of the large sensor, which also brings greater dynamic range (page 102) and better quality at high ISO ratings, extending the possibilities for shooting in low light.

Another plus is the D5300's ability to use the entire array of Nikon-fit lenses (see chapter 7, page 184): in particular, it can use wide-angle lenses which go well beyond the range of most camcorders. In addition, the full range of exposure settings, Nikon Picture Controls, and many other options can be used, giving a high level of creative control.

Limitations

The D5300's Movie mode is among the best on current DSLRs, but some limitations remain. The rear screen and the overall balance of a DSLR make handheld shooting awkward, though the fold-out screen does give the D5XXX series an edge over other Nikon models. There are now many accessory grips and supports to improve handling and stability.

Also, Live View AF is nowhere near agile enough for fast-moving subjects, and sound quality from the built-in microphone is at best moderate (*see page 174*).

There's one other limitation: you cannot record a clip longer than 20 minutes in High quality or 30 minutes in Normal quality. This is hardly ever a problem—and for those who have to view your movies, 20 minutes will seem like a very long time for a single clip!

Note:
Most digital video cameras claim enormous zoom ranges (often 800x or more) but these are only achieved by "digital zoom", which is a software function that enlarges the central portion of the image—inevitably losing quality. "Optical zoom" range is what matters, and interchangeable lenses give a potential range of at least 80x (10mm–800mm). The widest range currently available in a single lens is 18–300mm.

WIDE VIEW ❯❯
The D5300 allows wide-angle shooting.

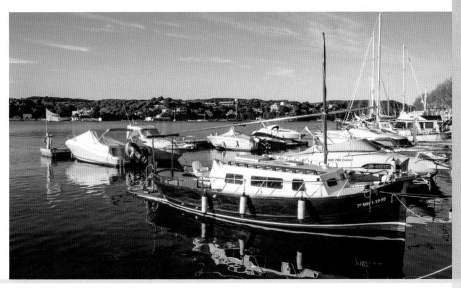

6 » MAKING MOVIES

› Preparation

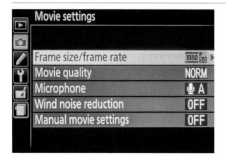

MOVIE SETTINGS ⌃

Before shooting, select key settings in the **Movie settings** section of the Shooting menu (see below). Other settings such as Picture Controls should also be set in advance (if using P, S, A, M exposure modes). A good way to check the general look of a shot is by taking a still frame— you can do this from Live View without starting movie recording first.

Quality sets the image size, frame rate, and quality for movie recording. The size options are: **1920 x 1080** pixels (default); **1280 x 720** pixels; **640 x 424** pixels. The frame rate options vary according to the size chosen and whether NTSC or PAL (*see page 125*) is selected for video mode.

Movie quality sets the compression level; options are High or Normal.

Microphone determines the sensitivity of the built-in microphone (or an external

microphone if attached). The options are: **Auto**, **Manual Sensitivity** (in steps from 1–20), and **Off**. You can see an audio-level display while in this menu, which helps to establish a correct setting.

> ### Tip
>
> *You can't change Manual microphone level settings while actually shooting a clip: this is another setting that needs to be sorted beforehand.*

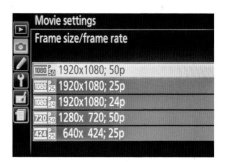

SETTING FRAME SIZE/FRAME RATE IN ⌃
THE MOVIE SETTINGS MENU

If you set **Manual movie** settings to **On**, you can adjust shutter speed while actually shooting a clip in M mode. You can also change ISO settings, not while actually shooting but at least without exiting Live

View. By default **Manual movie settings** is **Off**. When it is, you can dial in changes to the settings but they have no effect.

Whether this is **On** or **Off**, if you're shooting in M mode, you can't change the aperture without exiting Live View.

› Focus options

The focus modes and AF-area options for movie shooting are the same as for Live View (*page 89*). If Full-time servo AF (AF-F) is selected, the D5300 will automatically maintain focus while movie recording is in progress, though it may lag behind rapid camera/subject movements. If Single-servo AF (AF-S) is selected the camera will only refocus when you half-press the shutter-release button, and this is often all too obvious in the final movie clip.

Manual focusing is also possible, but can be yet another recipe for wobbly pictures. Again, this means the use of a tripod is recommended, especially with longer lenses, when focusing is more critical and wobbles are magnified. Some lenses have a smoother manual focus action than others. The physical design of older lenses often makes them more suitable, with large and well-placed focus rings.

DEPTH OF FIELD ❯❯
It's much easier to get shallow depth of field with the D5300 than with most video cameras.

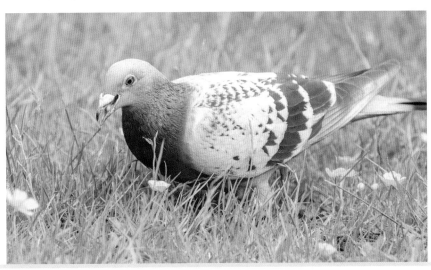

6

Older lenses often have a distance scale marked on the lens barrel, which can offer a viable alternative to using the Live View display to focus.

Study the credits for major movies and TV shows and you'll often see someone called a "focus puller". This is an assistant camera operator, whose sole task is to adjust the focus, normally between predetermined points (for instance shifting from one character's face to another). This leaves the lead camera operator free to concentrate on framing, panning, and/or zooming. Frequently, the focus puller uses the distance scale on the lens barrel, relying on previously measured distances. Executing this kind of deliberate and controlled focus shift is not easy, especially when you're the sole camera operator—and if it's not right, it will be very obvious in the final footage.

All of this suggests that changing focus during the shooting of a clip is potentially tricky. If not done smoothly and accurately it can also be very disconcerting when viewing the footage. And changing focus during shooting is often not necessary anyway. Using a fixed focus for each shot is often perfectly viable, especially when depth of field is good.

The best way to do this is by focusing manually before shooting. Alternatively, use AF and then change the focus mode to manual. A third option is to keep half-pressure on the shutter-release button to lock focus while shooting, but this may seem like an unnecessary hassle.

› Exposure

Exposure control depends on the exposure mode selected before shooting begins. If Auto or Scene modes are selected, exposure control is fully automatic, except that exposure level can be locked (in Scene modes) using the **AE-L/AF-L** button. This is useful, for instance, to prevent the main subject appearing to darken if it moves in front of a brighter background.

In P, S, or A mode, exposure levels can be adjusted by ±3 Ev using the 🔳 button. In addition, in A mode, aperture can be manually adjusted during shooting. Normally the camera will set the shutter speed automatically, and adjust the ISO sensitivity if necessary to keep shutter speed within suitable limits.

In mode M, and providing the Manual movie settings option (*see page 170*) is **On**, shutter speed can be adjusted "live" while shooting. In this case, also, ISO sensitivity is not adjusted automatically.

While all these adjustment options are welcome, actually making them while shooting is fiddly. It's hard to avoid jogging the camera unless it's on a very solid tripod, and the built-in microphone may also pick up the sounds of the operations. Another consequence can be abrupt brightness changes in the final footage.

It's nearly always better to get the settings right before you start shooting a clip.

› Shutter speed

You can (if the light's good) set shutter speeds right up to 1/4000 sec., but there are inevitable limits to the slowest speed you can select. For instance, if frame rate is 24, 25 or 30, the slowest possible speed is 1/30 sec. After all, if you're shooting 25 frames a second you can't expect each frame to have a ½ sec. exposure.

Based on still photography experience, you'll probably expect faster shutter speeds to give sharper pictures. In movies it doesn't work that way. If you shoot at, say, 1/500 sec., you will find that each frame of the movie might appear sharp when examined individually, but the motion appears jerky when you play the movie. This is because you have recorded 25 tiny slices of the continuous action. 25 times 1/500 sec. is just 5% of the action. The nearer the shutter speed is to 1/25 sec., the nearer you get to capturing 100% and the smoother the motion appears.

However, in bright conditions, you can't shoot at 1/25 sec. and at the same time use a really wide aperture for shallow depth of field, even at ISO 100. Sometimes you need to compromise, though a neutral density filter (*see page 209*) could come in handy.

LOW LIGHT ❯❯
The D5300 also scores when it comes to shooting in low-light conditions.

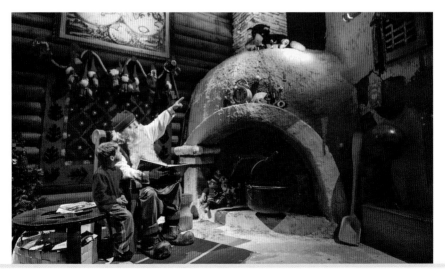

6 › Sound

The D5300's built-in microphone gives modest quality stereo output. It is liable to pick up any sounds you make during operation (focusing, zooming, even breathing). You always have the option to add a new soundtrack later. However, this is difficult if your film includes people speaking (though "post-syncing" is standard practice in Hollywood, especially for musicals). If you want to include dialog or "talking heads", keep subjects close to the camera and ensure that background noise is minimized.

Fortunately the D5300 also allows you to attach an external microphone: plug it in to a standard 3.5mm mini-jack socket under the cover on the left side of the camera. This automatically overrides the internal microphone.

Tip

Video shooting is a real drain on the battery. If you plan to spend a full day shooting movie clips, then you'll probably need several spare batteries, or a mains adapter (page 212) if you have access to mains power.

OUT ON THE RESERVE ❯❯
When shooting away from mains power, make sure you have ample battery reserves.

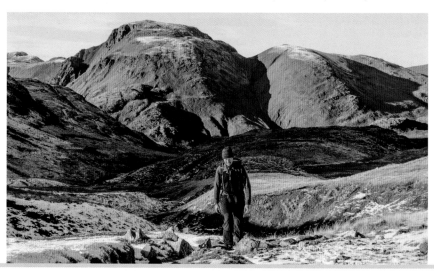

» SHOOTING MOVIES

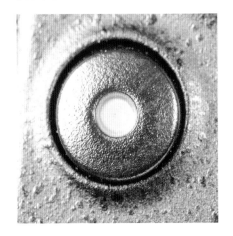

⦿ **BUTTON**   ⌃

1) Choose exposure mode, AF mode, and AF-area mode as for Live View shooting. If using A or M exposure mode, set the aperture. If using S mode, or M mode with Manual movie settings On, set the shutter speed.

2) Activate Live View by flicking the `Lv` switch. It's a good idea to go to the "movie indicators" screen by pressing **INFO** one or more times (*see page 89*).

3) Check framing and initial exposure level (possibly taking a still frame or very short clip as a test). Set initial focus by half-pressure on the shutter-release button, or focus manually.

4) Press ⦿ to start recording the movie. **REC** flashes on the monitor screen while recording, and an indicator shows the maximum remaining shooting time.

5) To stop recording, press ⦿ again.

6) Exit Live View by flicking `Lv`.

> ### *Tip*
>
> *To take a still photo during movie shooting, press the shutter-release button and keep it pressed until you hear the shutter operate (you may have to wait a second or so). Still frames can also be extracted from movies after shooting, but only at the current movie resolution (i.e. maximum 1920 x 1080 pixels).*

› Shooting

The golden rule is: think ahead. If a still frame isn't quite right, you can review it, change position or settings, and be ready to reshoot within seconds. To shoot and review even a short movie clip eats up much more time, and you may not get a second chance anyway. It's doubly important to get shooting position, framing, and camera settings right before you start. It's easy to check the general look of the shot by shooting a still frame beforehand, but this does not allow for movement of subject, camera, or both. You can also do a rehearsal in Live View before shooting for real.

If you're new to the complexities of movies, start with simple shots. Don't try zooming, panning, and focusing simultaneously: do one at a time. Many moving subjects can be filmed very well with a fixed camera: waterfalls, birds at a feeder, musicians playing, and loads more. Equally, you can become familiar with camera movements shooting static subjects: try panning across a wide landscape or zooming in from a broad cityscape to a detail of a single building.

› Handheld or tripod shooting

It's impossible to overstress the importance of a tripod for shooting decent movies. Shooting movie clips handheld is a good way to reveal just how wobbly you really are—especially as you can't use the Viewfinder. VR lens technology can counteract short-frequency shake, but does nothing to eliminate slower (and often larger) movements. Unless you're a Zen master, you cannot hold the camera perfectly still.

Of course, even "real" movie directors sometimes use handheld cameras to create a specific feel, but there's a huge difference between controlled movement for deliberate effect, and incessant, uncontrolled wobbliness. Using a tripod, or other suitable camera support, is the simplest way to give movie clips a polished, professional, look.

In the last few years we've also seen lots of new devices intended to stabilize the camera when you simply have to shoot handheld, from simple brackets to smaller versions of the legendary Steadicam. If none of these are available, look for other alternatives, for instance by sitting with elbows braced on knees. For moving shots, too, improvisation can pay dividends; for instance, I've seen a tripod mounted in the bed of an old-style pram, whose large wheels and sprung body gave a remarkably smooth result in a tracking shot.

Whatever you do, for whatever kind of shot, the golden rule is "think steady".

Tip

A standard tripod with a pan-and-tilt head is a good start. If you're serious about movies, consider buying a dedicated video tripod (or tripod head). This isn't necessarily heftier than its standard counterpart, but the tripod head is specifically designed to move smoothly.

› Panning

The panning shot is a movie-maker's staple. Often essential for following moving subjects, it can also be used with static subjects, for instance, sweeping across a vast panorama. Of course, landscapes aren't always static, and a panning shot combined with breaking waves, running water, or grass blowing in the breeze can produce beautiful results.

Handheld panning is very problematic; it may be acceptable when following a moving subject, but a wobbly pan across a grand landscape will definitely grate. You really, really need a tripod for this—and make sure it's properly levelled, or you may start panning with the camera aimed at the horizon but finish seeing nothing but ground or sky: do a "dry-run" before shooting.

Keep panning movements slow and steady. Panning too rapidly can make the shot hard to "read" and even leave viewers feeling nauseous. Smooth panning is easiest with video tripods, but perfectly possible with a standard model: leave the pan adjustment slightly slack.

ON THE LEVEL ⌄⌄
When panning on a tripod, get it levelled correctly in advance, or the train could appear to be on a much steeper slope than any normal railway.

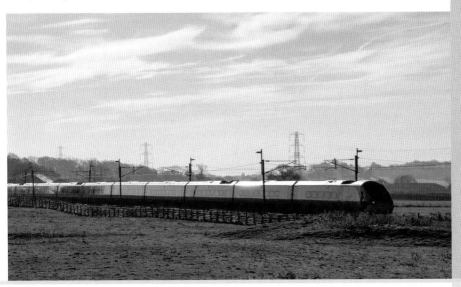

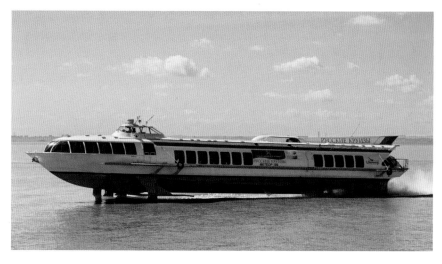

PANNING
This is a classic panning shot, but very tricky to follow neatly when handholding—especially as I was on a similar vessel going the other way.

Hold the panning arm on the tripod head, not the camera, and use the front of the lens as a reference to track steadily across the scene.

With moving subjects, the speed and direction of panning is dictated by the need to keep the subject in frame. Accurate tracking of fast-moving subjects is very challenging and takes a lot of practice.

› Zooming

The zoom is another fundamental technique. Moving from a wide view to a tighter one is called zooming in, the converse zooming out. Again, a little forethought makes all the difference to using the zoom effectively; consider the framing of the shot at both start and finish. If you're zooming in to a specific subject, double-check it's central in the frame.

No current lenses for the D5300 are designed specifically for shooting movies—this is most obvious in relation to zooming. Firstly, none of them have such a wide zoom range as video camera lenses. More seriously, it's hard to achieve a really smooth, even-paced zoom action. Practice does help, and firmly mounting the

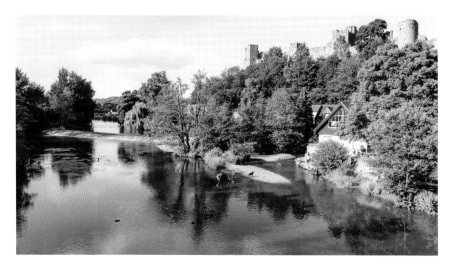

The camera can "explore" a scene like this, either by panning around to see more of the setting or by zooming in for a closer look. But it wouldn't do to zoom too far here, as the center of the frame is occupied by foliage (unless you can tilt the camera at the same time—a hard act to pull off on anything but a true video tripod).

camera on a solid tripod helps even more. Zooming while handholding virtually guarantees jerky zoom and overall wobbliness. It's also worth experimenting to see which lens has the smoothest zoom action. There's definitely a gap in the market for a lens with wide focal length-range and powered zoom.

When zooming, remember that depth of field (*see page 60*) decreases at the telephoto end of the range. Your subject may appear perfectly sharp in a wide-angle view but end up looking soft when you zoom in. Set focus at the telephoto end, whether your planned shot involves zooming out or zooming in.

› Lighting

For obvious reasons, you can't use flash. There are now many LED light units specifically designed for DSLR-movie shooting. The D5300's ability to shoot at high ISO ratings is also invaluable.

› Still frame capture

To capture a still frame during movie shooting, simply press the shutter-release button. This will end movie-recording, take the shot and return you to Live View. The resulting image will use the 16:9 aspect ratio; quality and size are determined by your still-image settings (*see pages 79–80*). For image sizes see the table below.

You can also extract a still frame from a movie clip you've already shot, but don't expect too much. The image size will be the same as your selected movie frame size (1920 x 1080, 1280 x 720 or 640 x 424 pixels) and motion which appears smooth when playing the movie may well look blurred in the single frame.

STILL WATER   ⌄
You can capture a still frame while shooting a movie, but the settings may not be what you'd choose when shooting a standalone photo.

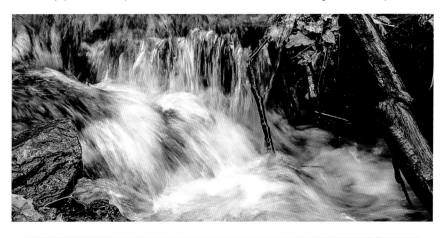

Image area	Image size setting	Size in pixels
DX movie	Large (or RAW)	6000 x 3368
	Medium	4496 x 2528
	Small	2992 x 1680
1.3x crop	Large (or RAW)	4800 x 2696
	Medium	3600 x 2024
	Small	2400 x 1344

» EDITING

The D5300 doesn't shoot movies. Like all movie cameras, it shoots movie clips. In general, turning a collection of clips into a movie that people actually want to see requires editing, and specifically Non-Linear Editing (NLE). This simply means that clips in the final movie don't have to appear in the same order in which they were shot. Digital editing is also non-destructive—this means that it does not affect your original clips (unlike cutting and splicing bits of film in the "old days"). During editing, you manipulate preview versions of these clips and the software merely keeps "notes" on the edit. At the end, you export the result as a new movie—remember that this can take a long time to "render".

› Software

Nikon now provides movie editing software for Mac and Windows as part of the View NX2 suite provided with the camera. Nikon Movie Editor is a basic, simple editing package but it handles all the key tasks.

Other, more sophisticated options are also available at no cost. Mac users have iMovie, part of the iLife suite, included with all new Macs. The Windows equivalent is Windows Movie Maker, pre-installed with Windows Vista, and a free download from

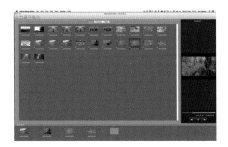

NIKON MOVIE EDITOR ⌃

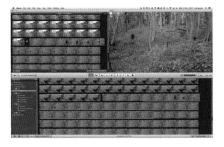

IMOVIE ⌃

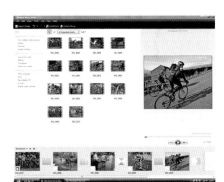

WINDOWS MOVIE MAKER ⌃

6

windowslive.com for Windows 7 or 8. A more advanced (but not free) option, for either platform, is Adobe Premiere Elements.

All these apps make it easy to trim and reorder your original clips. Instead of simply cutting instantaneously between shots, you can apply various transitions such as dissolves, wipes, and fades. You can also adjust the look of any clip or segment of the movie; as well as basic controls for brightness, color, and so on. A range of special effects can be added: you can, for instance, make your movie look scratched and faded, as if shot on film 50 years ago rather than yesterday with a DSLR.

You can also add other media, like still photos and sound. You can insert stills individually at appropriate points or create slideshows within the main movie. Again, effects and transitions can be applied to give slideshows a more dynamic feel.

It's equally easy to add a new soundtrack, like a voiceover or music, to part or all of the movie. Last but not least, you can also add titles and captions.

› Taking it further

There's far more to movie-making than we can cover in a single chapter. A useful next step would be *Understanding HD Video* by Chiz Dakin, from this publisher.

Tips

If you haven't created them yourself, all photos, music, and other media are someone else's copyright. Look for open-source material or get the copyright owner's permission to use their work.

Effects and transitions are great fun—and non-destructive editing means you can experiment to your heart's content—but, for the sake of the audience, it's best to use a limited selection in the final version.

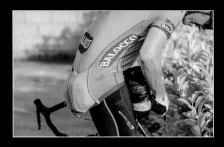 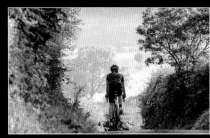

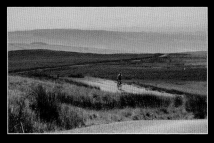 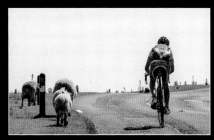

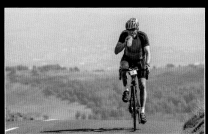 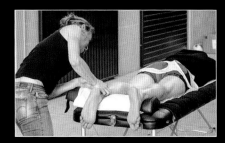

STORYTELLING

When you're shooting stills, a single image may have tremendous power and impact. In video, one shot is hardly ever enough, and instead you have to think about different shots and how they relate to each other to tell a story.

7 LENSES

There are many reasons to choose an SLR like the D5300. One of the most important is the ability to use a vast range of lenses, including Nikon's own legendary system as well as lenses from other makers. Even the growing band of compact system ("mirrorless") cameras don't have access to such a wide choice.

Nikon's F-mount lens mount is now 50 years old, though it has evolved in that time. Still, most Nikkor lenses will fit the D5300, and work (albeit sometimes with major limitations). However, there are still sound reasons why more recent lenses are most suitable, notably that many older lenses cannot autofocus on the D5300—see Loss of functions, below.

Another reason for preferring lenses designed specifically for digital cameras relates to the way light reaches the minute individual photodiodes or "photosites" on the camera's sensor. Because these are slightly recessed, there can be some cut-off if light hits them at an angle. This is less critical with film, for which older Nikkor lenses were designed. Many older lenses can still be used, and can give very good results, but critical examination may show some peripheral loss of brightness (vignetting), and perhaps a hint of chromatic aberration (color fringing). Wide-angle lenses are usually most susceptible. Much depends on the size of print or reproduction you require, and these shortcomings can to some extent

be corrected in post-processing (especially if you shoot RAW).

Nikon's DX-series and other newer lenses are specifically designed for digital cameras, maintaining illumination and image quality right across the frame. DX lenses are therefore listed first in the table of Nikkor lenses on *pages 202–207*.

› Loss of functions

When older lenses are used on the Nikon D5300, many functions may be lost. In particular, autofocus is only available with lenses with a built-in motor. Suitable Nikon lenses are designated AF-I or AF-S. Check carefully when considering lenses from independent makers (for instance, with Sigma lenses, look for the "HSM" tag).

Other AF lenses with a built-in CPU will support some or all of the camera's metering functions and exposure modes, but will require manual focusing. The electronic rangefinder (*see page 74*) can be helpful.

Older lenses without a built-in CPU, such as AI and AI-S types, can be attached, but the camera's metering will not operate. You'll need to use exposure mode M—set aperture and shutter speed using an external meter or by trial and error, and use Image review (*page 108*) to check exposure. When using flash or indoor lighting, the same settings can often be used repeatedly.

› Nikon lens technology

Nikon lenses have a high reputation, and many incorporate special features or materials. As these are referred to extensively in the table on *pages 202–207*, brief explanations of the main terms and acronyms are given here.

Warning!

Some older lenses, specifically pre-AI lenses, should not be used as they can damage the camera. Certain other specific (and uncommon) lenses should also be avoided—see the *Nikon Reference Manual*. At the time of writing there are reports of compatibility issues between the D5300 and many Sigma lenses, affecting both AF performance and image stabilization. To fix this requires a lens firmware update. Newly-purchased lenses should have current firmware.

Abbreviation	Term	Explanation
AF	Autofocus	Lens focuses automatically. The majority of current Nikkor lenses are AF but a substantial manual focus range remains.
ASP	Aspherical Lens Elements	Precisely configured lens elements that reduce the incidence of certain aberrations. Especially useful in reducing distortion with wide-angle lenses.
CRC	Close-range Correction	Advanced lens design that improves picture quality at close focusing distances.
D	Distance	Types D and G lenses communicate information to the camera about the distance at which they are focusing, supporting functions such as 3D Matrix Metering.

7

DC	Defocus-Image Control	Found in a few lenses aimed mostly at portrait photographers; allows control of aberrations and thereby appearance of out-of-focus areas in the image.
DX	DX lens	Lenses specifically designed for DX-format digital cameras (see introduction to this chapter).
G	Type G lens	Modern Nikkor lenses with no aperture ring; aperture must be set by the camera.
ED	Extra-low Dispersion	ED glass minimizes chromatic aberration (the tendency for light of different colors to be focused at slightly different points).
IF	Internal Focusing	Only internal elements of the lens move during focusing: the front element does not extend or rotate.
M/A	Manual/Auto	Many Nikkor AF lenses offer M/A mode, allowing seamless transition from automatic to manual focusing.
N	Nano Crystal Coat	Said to virtually eliminate internal reflections within lenses, minimizing flare.
RF	Rear Focusing	Lens design where only the rearmost elements move during focusing; makes AF operation faster.
SIC	Super Integrated Coating	Nikon-developed lens coating that minimizes flare and "ghosting".
SWM	Silent Wave Motor	Special in-lens motors which deliver very fast and very quiet autofocus operation.
VR	Vibration Reduction	System which compensates for camera shake. VR is said to allow handheld shooting up to three stops slower than would otherwise be possible (i.e. 1/15th instead of 1/125 sec.). New lenses now feature VRII, said to gain an extra stop over VR (1/8th instead of 1/125 sec.).

» FOCAL LENGTH

A prime lens has a fixed focal length and, of course, a zoom lens has variable focal length. Though familiar, the term "focal length" is often misapplied. The focal length of any lens is a fundamental optical property, and is not changed by fitting the lens to a different camera. Unfortunately, as if to promote confusion, the lenses on most digital compact cameras are described not by their actual focal length but by their "35mm equivalent"—i.e. the focal length that would give the same angle of view on a 35mm or full-frame camera. However, an 18–55mm zoom is always an 18–55 zoom, regardless of whether it's fitted on a DX-format camera like the D5300 or a full-frame (FX) camera like the D800. However, because the D5300 has a smaller sensor than the D800, the image that's captured shows a smaller field of view.

FX/DX IMAGE AREA   ❯❯
The original was shot with a 24mm lens on a Nikon D700. The red rectangle shows the area that would be captured using the same lens, from the same position, on a DX camera like the D5300.

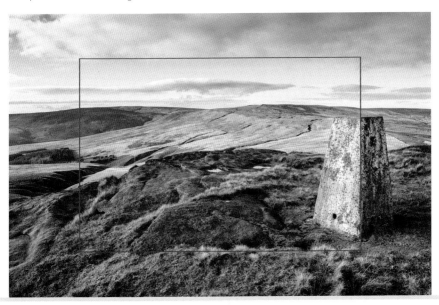

› Field of view

The field of view, or angle of view, is the area covered by the image frame. While the focal length of a lens remains the same on any camera, the angle of view seen in the image is different for different sensor formats. The angle of view is usually measured on the diagonal of the frame (as in the table on *pages 202–207*).

› Crop factor

The D5300's smaller sensor, relative to the 35mm/FX standard, means that it has a crop factor, or focal length magnification factor, of 1.5. If you fit a 200mm lens to a D5300, the field of view equates to what you'd see with a 300mm lens on a full-frame camera (e.g. D4 or D600). For sports and wildlife this can be an advantage, allowing long-range shooting with relatively light and inexpensive lenses. Conversely, the crop factor makes wide-angle lenses effectively less wide, which is unwelcome news for landscape shooters. However, this has fostered the development of new ultra-wide lenses, like the 10–24mm f/3.5–4.5G DX Nikkor.

The page opposite shows a series of images taken on a Nikon D5300, from a fixed position, with lenses from 12mm to 300mm.

> ### *Tip*
>
> *Throughout this book, and specifically in the shooting details for the photos, the true focal length is used.*

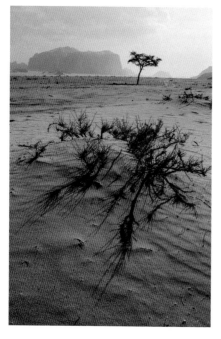

DESERT ⌃
A wide-angle lens helps to accentuate the vastness of the desert in this shot. *18mm, 1/125 sec., f/13, ISO 250.*

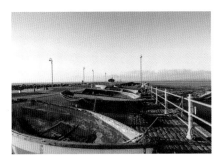
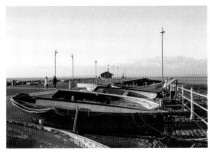
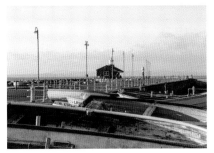
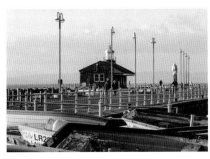
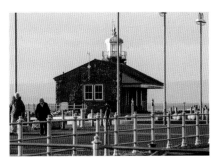
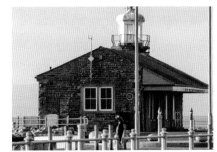

PIER REVIEW ⌃
The same scene shot with lenses of different focal lengths (from top left): *12mm, 24mm, 50mm, 100mm, 200mm, 300mm. 1/125 sec., f/11, ISO 200.*

7 » PERSPECTIVE

Perspective concerns the visual relationship between objects at different distances. The apparent fading of distant objects due to haze is atmospheric perspective, while optical perspective relates to the changes in apparent size of objects at different distances.

It's often stated that different lenses give different perspective. This is wrong: perspective is determined purely by distance. However, different lenses do lend themselves to different working distances and therefore are often associated with different perspectives.

A strong emphasis on the foreground may be called "wide-angle perspective" because a wide-angle lens allows you to move closer to foreground objects. Similarly, the apparent compression of perspective in telephoto shots is a result of the greater working distance with the long lens.

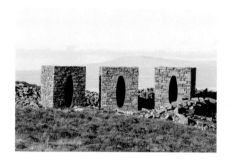

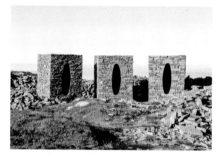

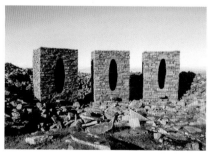

PERSPECTIVE »
In this series of shots (taken with, from top to bottom, 170mm, 55mm, and 18mm lenses) the structures remain the same apparent size even though viewed from different distances, but their apparent shape and their relationship to the background change radically. *1/160 sec., f/11, ISO 200, tripod.*

» LENS ISSUES

› Flare

Lens flare is usually seen when shooting towards the sun or other bright light sources. Caused by reflections within the lens, it may produce a string of colored blobs or a more general "veiling" effect.

Advanced lens coatings help reduce flare, as does keeping lenses and filters clean. Even so, when the sun's directly in shot, some flare may be inescapable. You can sometimes mask the sun, perhaps behind a tree.

If the sun isn't actually in shot, you can shield the lens. A good lens hood is essential, but may need to be supplemented with a piece of card, a map, or your hand. This is easier when using a

tripod; otherwise it requires assistance, or one-handed shooting. Check carefully to see if the flare has gone—and that the shading object hasn't crept into shot!

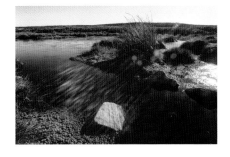

FLARE »
The flare in the first shot (top right) is all too obvious, but was eliminated in the second by carefully shading the lens. *12mm, 1/250 sec., f/11, ISO 200.*

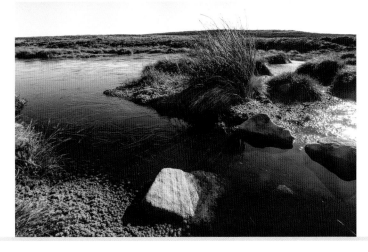

› Distortion

Distortion makes lines which are really straight appear curved in the image. Distortion is usually worst with zoom lenses, especially at the extremes of the zoom range. When straight lines bow outwards, it's called barrel distortion; when they bend inwards, it's called pincushion distortion. Distortion often goes unnoticed when shooting natural subjects with no straight lines, but can still rear its ugly head when level horizons appear in landscape or seascape images.

Distortion can be corrected using **Auto Distortion Control** in the Shooting menu; this requires a compatible lens and only works on JPEG images. It can also be tackled using **Distortion Control** in the Retouch menu or in post-processing. However, remember that all these methods crop the image.

› Chromatic aberration

Chromatic aberration occurs when light of different colors is focused in slightly different places on the sensor, and appears as colored fringing when images are examined closely. The D5300 has built-in correction for chromatic aberration during processing of JPEG images. Aberration can also be corrected in post-processing; with RAW images this is the only option.

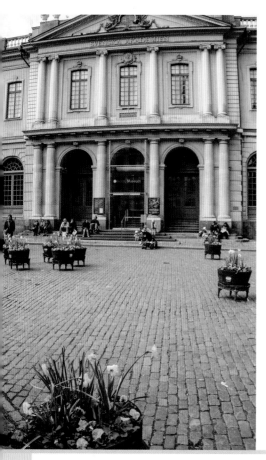

DISTORTION   **«**
Distortion was exaggerated in post-processing—it's all too obvious in the upper part of the building. *18mm, 1/125 sec., f/13, ISO 250.*

› Vignetting

Vignetting is a darkening towards the corners of the image, most conspicuous in even-toned areas like clear skies. Most lenses show slight vignetting at maximum aperture, but it should reduce on stopping down. Like most faults, it can be tackled in post-processing. Severe vignetting can arise if you use unsuitable lens hoods and filter holders, or "stack" multiple filters on the lens.

› Lens care

Lenses require special care. Glass elements and coatings are easily scratched and this will degrade your images. Remove dust and dirt with a blower. Fingerprints and other marks should be removed using a dedicated lens cleaner and optical grade cloth. A skylight or UV filter (*see page 208*) will help protect the lens, and lens caps should be replaced when the lens is not in use.

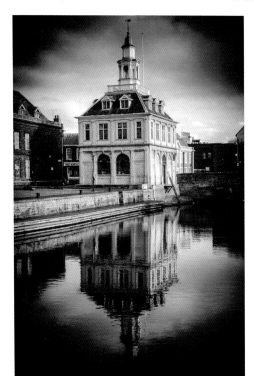

VIGNETTE   «
A strong vignette effect was added in post-processing; along with the monochrome treatment, it gives this recent digital shot an antique look. *38mm, 1/160 sec., f/11, ISO 400.*

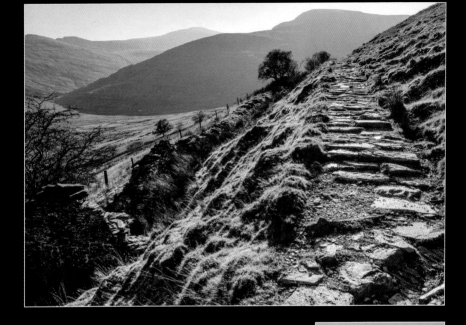

THE RIGHT TRACK

Photographing this track and the surrounding landscape,
there is no single localized "subject" and I knew that the
result would look unnatural if any part of the image ended
up unsharp. The combination of a short focal length, a
fairly small aperture, and a focus point in the middle of the
track ensured that depth of field covered everything.

Settings
> ISO 250
> 1/320 sec. at f/11
> 18mm lens

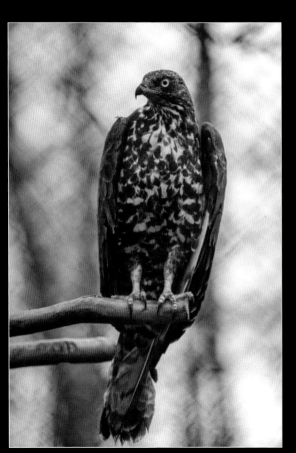

NET EFFECT

Limited depth of field
is often inescapable
in wildlife shots. In this
case, as the bird was
in an enclosure, it also
helped to throw the
netting in the background
out of focus.

Settings
> ISO 250
> 1/640 sec. at f/3.5
> 200mm lens

7 » LENS TYPES

› Standard lenses

In traditional 35mm photography (and full-frame digital), a 50mm lens is called standard, as its field of view is held to approximate that of the human eye—this is debatable, but the label has stuck. Because of the crop factor of the D5300, the equivalent lens would be around 35mm. Standard lenses are typically light, simple, and have wide maximum apertures. Zoom lenses whose range covers the 35mm focal length are often referred to as "standard zooms".

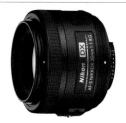

NIKKOR 50MM F/1.8 ☆

CASTLE VIEW ☽
Although a standard lens may not be the natural choice for landscape shots, it provides a field of view considered to be the closest to the human eye. *42mm, 1/200 sec., f/11, ISO 200.*

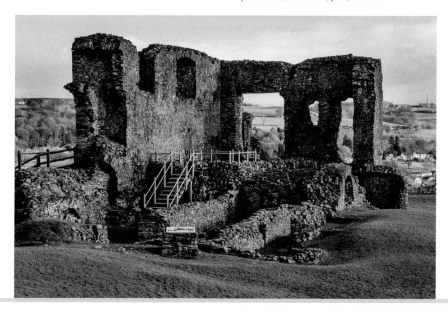

› Wide-angle lenses

A wide-angle lens is any lens wider than a standard lens; for the D5300 this means any lens shorter than 35mm. Wide-angle lenses are valuable for working close to subjects or bringing foregrounds into greater prominence. They lend themselves both to photographing expansive scenic views and to working in cramped spaces where you can't step back to "get more in". With the D5300's crop factor, a lens like an 18mm, once regarded as "super-wide", gives a less extreme angle of view. Wider lenses like Nikon's 12-24mm are now available.

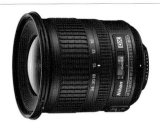

10-24MM F/3.5-4.5G DX NIKKOR   ≪

LAKE PLACID   ≫
A wide-angle lens offers the broad field of view necessary for capturing landscape shots. *14mm, 1/13 sec., f/11, ISO 100, tripod.*

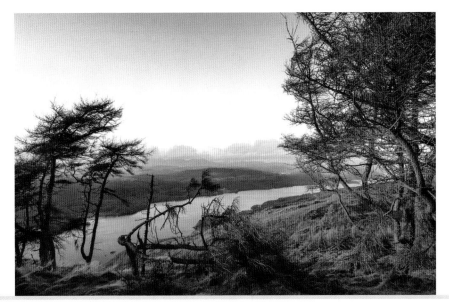

› Telephoto lenses

Telephoto lenses, often simply called long lenses, give a narrow angle of view. They are mostly employed when working distances need to be longer, as in wildlife and sports photography, but have many other uses, such as singling out small and/or distant elements in a landscape. Moderate telephoto lenses are favored for portrait photography, because the greater working distance gives a natural-looking result and is more comfortable for nervous subjects. The traditional "portrait" range is 85–135mm, equivalent to using lenses of around 60–90mm with the D5300.

The laws of optics, combined with greater working distances, mean depth

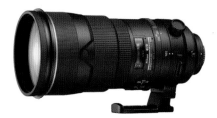

NIKKOR 300MM F/2.8G ED VR II AF-S ⌄

of field is limited. This is often beneficial in portraiture, wildlife, and sport, as it concentrates attention on the subject by throwing backgrounds out of focus. It can be less welcome in landscape shooting.

The size and weight of longer lenses make them harder to handhold comfortably, and their narrow angle of view also magnifies any movement; high shutter speeds and/or the use of a tripod or other camera support are therefore the order of the day. Nikon's Vibration Reduction (VR) technology also mitigates the effects of camera shake—but it can slow down the maximum frame rate, a factor sports shooters in particular need to recognize.

EYE-TO-EYE ⌄
Wildlife photographers favor telephoto lenses for getting close to the subject without causing unnecessary disturbance. *180mm, 1/400 sec., f/2.8, ISO 400.*

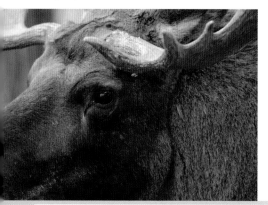

> ### *Tip*
>
> *Switch VR OFF when using the camera on a tripod. Otherwise, it can sometimes add shake instead of removing it.*

› Zoom lenses

The term "zoom" covers lenses with variable focal length, like the AF-S DX Nikkor 18–105mm f/3.5-5.6G. A zoom lens can replace a bagful of prime lenses and cover the gaps in between, scoring highly for weight, convenience, and economy. Flexible focal length also allows very precise framing.

While once considered inferior in optical quality, there is now little to choose between a good zoom and a good prime lens, at least in terms of general sharpness and contrast. Most zoom lenses will have a "sweet spot" somewhere in the zoom range where distortion is minimal, but many show discernible barrel distortion at wide settings and pincushion at the long end.

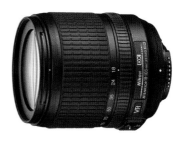

ZOOM-NIKKOR 18–105MM F/3.5–5.6G ✖
AF-S VR

Zooms with a very wide range (e.g. 18–200mm or 28–300mm) may still be optically compromised, and usually have a relatively small ("slow") maximum aperture, but they are undeniably versatile. That wide, uninterrupted zoom range can prove useful for movie shooting in particular.

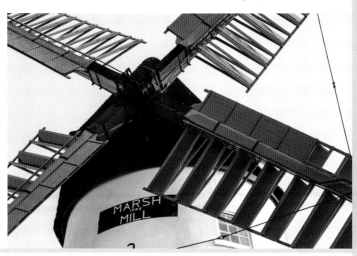

WINDMILL »
A zoom lens's versatility helps with creative photography, offering the chance to try different shots of the same subject at different focal lengths from the same spot. *66mm, 1/250 sec., f/8, ISO 200.*

7

› Perspective control lenses

Perspective control (PC or "tilt-and-shift") lenses give unique flexibility in viewing and controlling the image. Their most obvious application is in photographing architecture, where with a "normal" lens it often becomes necessary to tilt the camera upwards, resulting in converging verticals (buildings appear to lean back or even to one side). The shift function allows the camera back to be kept vertical, which in turn means that vertical lines in the subject remain vertical in the image. Tilt movements also allow extra control over depth of field, whether to extend or to minimize it.

The Nikon range features three PC lenses, with focal lengths of 24mm, 45mm, and 85mm. They retain many automatic functions, but require manual focusing.

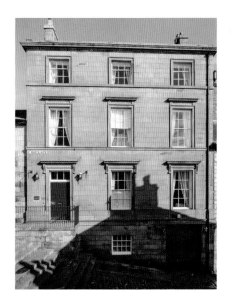

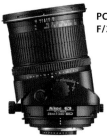

**PC-E NIKKOR 24MM ‹‹
F/3.5D ED**

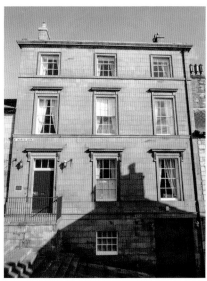

STRAIGHT-SHOOTING »
Looking steeply up with a normal lens, the convergence of vertical lines is obvious (right). It can be corrected but this crops the image. A perspective control lens (top right) avoids this. *24mm, 1/200 sec., f/10, ISO 200.*

› Macro lenses

For specialist close-up work there is little to beat a true macro lens. For more on these *see page 165.*

› Teleconverters

Teleconverters are supplementary optics which fit between the main lens and the camera body, and magnify the focal length of the main lens. Nikon currently offers the TC-14E II (1.4x magnification), TC-17E II (1.7x), and TC-20E II (2x). The advantages are obvious, allowing you to extend the focal length range with minimal additional weight (the TC-14E II, for example, weighs just 7oz or 200 grams).

However, teleconverters can degrade image quality—as you might expect, the higher the magnification factor of the converter the more noticeable this is. The TC-20E III, in particular, produces a significant loss of sharpness, especially if you try and shoot at maximum aperture. Results improve when the lens is stopped down to f/8 or f/11—beyond this, sharpness tails off again due to diffraction.

Converters also cause a loss of light. Fitting a 2x converter to an f/4 lens turns it into an effective f/8. One consequence is that the camera's autofocus may become sluggish or will only work with the central focus points.

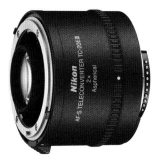

AF-S TELECONVERTER TC-20E III ⌃

COAST CLOSE-UP ⌄
A 2x converter doubles the focal length of your lens with minimum weight penalty. *110mm, 1/1600 sec., f/7.1, ISO 800.*

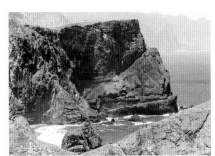

› Lens hoods

A lens hood serves two main functions: it shields the lens against knocks, rain, and other hazards; and excludes any stray light which does not contribute to the image but may degrade it by causing flare. Most Nikkor lenses come with a lens hood.

7 » NIKKOR LENS CHART

Optical features/notes

DX Lenses

Lens	Optical features/notes
10.5mm f/2.8G DX Fisheye	CRC
10–24mm f/3.5–4.5G ED AF-S DX	ED, IF, SWM
12–24mm f/4G ED-IF AF-S DX	SWM
16–85mm f/3.5–5.6G ED VR AF-S DX	VRII, SWM
17–55mm f/2.8G ED-IF AF-S DX	ED, SWM
18–55mm f/3.5–5.6G AF-S VR DX	VR, SWM
18-55 f/3.5–5.6GII AF-S DX	ED, SWM
18–70mm f/3.5–4.5G ED-IF AF-S DX	ED, SWM
18–105mm f/3.5–5.6G ED VR AF-S DX	ED, IF, VRII, NC, SWM
18–140mm F/3.5–5.6G ED VR AF-S DX	ED, IF, VRII, SWM
18–200mm f/3.5–5.6G ED AF-S VRII DX	ED, SWM, VRII
18–300mm f/3.5–5.6G ED VR AF-S DX	ED, IF, SWM, VRII
35mm f/1.8G AF-S	SWM
40mm f/2.8G AF-S DX Micro NIKKOR	SWM
55–200mm f/4–5.6 AF-S VR DX	ED, SWM, VR
55–200mm f/4–5.6G ED AF-S DX	ED, SWM
55–300mm f/4.5–5.6G ED VR	ED, SWM
85mm f/3.5G ED VR AF-S DX Micro Nikkor	ED, IF, SWM, VRII

AF Prime lenses

Lens	Optical features/notes
14mm f/2.8D ED AF	ED, RF
16mm f/2.8D AF Fisheye	CRC
20mm f/2.8D AF	CRC
24mm f/1.4G ED	ED, NC
24mm f/2.8D AF	

Angle of view on DX format	Minimum focus distance (m)	Filter size (mm)	Dimensions diameter x length (mm)	Weight (g)
180	0.14	Rear	63 x 62.5	300
109–61	0.24	77	82.5 x 87	460
99–61	0.3	77	82.5 x 90	485
83–18.5	0.38	67	72 x 85	485
79–28.5	0.36	77	85.5 x 11.5	755
76–28.5	0.28	52	73 x 79.5	265
76–28.5	0.28	52	70.5 x 74	205
76–22.5	0.38	67	73 x 75.5	420
76–15.3	0.45	67	76 x 89	420
76–11.5	0.45	67	78 x 97	490
76–8	0.5	72	77 x 96.5	560
76–5.3	0.45	77	83 x 120	830
44	0.3	52	70 x 52.5	210
38.5	0.163	52	68.5 x 64.5	235
28.5–8	1.1	52	73 x 99.5	335
28.5–8	0.95	52	68 x 79	255
28.5–5.2	1.4	58	76.5 x 123	530
18.5	0.28	52	73 x 98.5	355
90	0.2	Rear	87 x 86.5	670
120	0.25	Rear	63 x 57	290
70	0.25	62	69 x 42.5	270
61	0.25	77	83 x 88.5	620
61	0.3	52	64.5 x 46	270

Optical features/notes

28mm f/1.8G AF-S	NC, SWM
28mm f/2.8D AF	
35mm f/2D AF	
35mm f/1.4G AF-S	NC, SWM
50mm f/1.8G AF-S	SWM
50mm f/1.8D AF	
50mm f/1.4D AF	
50mm f/1.4G AF-S	IF, SWM
58mm f/1.4G AF-S	NC, SWM
85mm f/1.4G AF	SWM, NC
85mm f/1.8D AF	RF
105mm f/2D AF DC	DC
135mm f/2D AF DC	DC
180mm f/2.8D ED-IF AF	ED, IF
200mm f/2G ED-IF AF-S VRII	ED, VRII, SWM
300mm f/2.8G ED VR II AF-S	ED, VRII, NC, SWM
300mm f/4D ED-IF AF-S	ED, IF
400mm f/2.8G ED VR AF-S	ED, IF, VRII, NC
400mm f/2.8D ED-IF AF-S II	ED, SWM
500mm f/4G ED VR AF-S	IF, ED, VRII, NC
600mm f/4G ED VR AF-S	ED, IF, VRII, NC
800mm f/5.6E FL ED VR AF-S	ED, NC, SWM, FL

AF Zoom lenses

14–24mm f/2.8G ED AF-S	IF, ED, SWM, NC
16–35mm f/4G ED VR	NC, ED, VR

Angle of view on DX format	Minimum focus distance (m)	Filter size (mm)	Dimensions diameter x length (mm)	Weight (g)
53	0.25	67	73 x 80.5	330
53	0.25	52	65 x 44.5	205
44	0.25	52	64.5 x 43.5	205
44	0.3	67	83 x 89.5	600
31.3	0.45	58	72 x 52.5	185
31.3	0.45	52	63 x 39	160
31.3	0.45	52	64.5 x 42.5	230
31.3	0.45	58	73.5 x 54	280
27.3	0.58	72	85 x 70	385
18.5	0.85	77	86.5 x 84	595
18.5	0.85	62	71.5 x 58.5	380
15.2	0.9	72	79 x 111	640
12	1.1	72	79 x 120	815
9.1	1.5	72	78.5 x 144	760
8.2	1.9	52	124 x 203	2930
5.2	2.2	52	124 x 267.5	2900
5.2	1.45	77	90 x 222.5	1440
4	2.9	52	159.5 x 368	4620
4	3.8	52	160 x 352	4800
3.1	4	52	139.5 x 391	3880
2.4	5	52	166 x 445	5060
2	5.9	52	160 x 461	4590
90–61	0.28	None	98 x 131.5	970
83–44	0.29	77	82.5 x 125	745

Optical features/notes

17–35mm f/2.8D ED-IF AF-S	IF, ED, SWM
18–35mm f/3.5–4.5G ED AF-S	ED, SWM
24–70mm f/2.8G ED AF-S	ED, SWM, NC
24–85mm f/2.8–4D IF AF	
24–85mm f/3.5–4.5G ED VR AF-S	ED, VRII, SWM
24–120mm f/4G ED-IF AF-S VR	ED, SWM, NC, VRII
28–300mm f/3.5–5.6G ED VR	ED, SWM
70–200mm f/2.8G ED-IF AF-S VRII	ED, SWM, VRII
70–200mm f/4G ED AF-S VRIII	ED, IF, SWM, NC, VRIII
70–300mm f/4.5–5.6G AF-S VR	ED, IF, SWM, VRII
80–400mm f/4.5–5.6D ED VR AF	ED, VR
200–400mm f/4G ED-IF AF-S VRII	ED, NC, VRII, SWM

Macro lenses

60mm f/2.8G ED AF-S Micro	ED, SWM, NC
105mm f/2.8G AF-S VR Micro	ED, IF, VRII, NC, SWM
200mm f/4D ED-IF AF Micro	ED, CRC

Perspective control

24mm f/3.5D ED PC-E (manual focus)	ED, NC
45mm f/2.8D ED PC-E (manual focus)	ED, NC
85mm f/2.8D ED PC-E (manual focus)	ED, NC

Angle of view on DX format	Minimum focus distance (m)	Filter size (mm)	Dimensions diameter x length (mm)	Weight (g)
79–44	0.28	77	82.5 x 106	745
76–44	0.28	77	83 x 95	385
61–22.50	0.38	77	83 x 133	900
61–18.5	0.5	72	78.5 x 82.5	545
61–18.5	0.38	72	78 x 82	465
61–13.5	0.45	77	84 x 103.5	710
53–5.2	0.5	77	83 x 114.5	800
22.5–8	1.4	77	87 x 209	1540
22.5–8	1	67	78 x 178.5	850
22.5–5.20	1.5	67	80 x 143.5	745
20–4	2.3	77	91 x 171	1340
8–4	2	52	124 x 365.5	3360
26.3	0.185	62	73 x 89	425
15	0.31	62	83 x 116	720
8	0.5	62	76 x 104.5	1190
56	0.21	77	82.5 x 108	730
34.5	0.25	77	83.5 x 112	780
18.9	0.39	77	82.7 x 107	650

8 ACCESSORIES

Digital SLRs are system cameras: as well as lenses and flash units, there are many other accessories which can extend the capabilities of the camera. Nikon's system is huge, and third-party suppliers offer even more options.

» FILTERS

Some types of filter are virtually redundant with digital cameras; the white balance controls (*page 80*) have largely eliminated the need for color-correction filters, which were essential for accurate color on film, especially transparency film.

Avoid using filters unnecessarily. Adding extra layers of glass in front of the lens can degrade the image and increase flare (*see page 191*). There is one exception: keeping a UV or skylight filter (see below) attached to each lens provides a first line of defence against knocks and scratches.

› Types of filter

Filters can be attached to the lens in several ways. The most familiar type are circular filters which screw to the front of the lens. The filter-thread diameter (in mm) of most Nikon lenses is specified in the table on *pages 202–207*, and usually marked around the front of the lens next to a Ø symbol. Nikon produces high-quality filters in sizes matching Nikkor lenses; larger ranges come from Hoya and B+W.

If you use filters extensively, you'll find slot-in filters more economical and convenient. The square or rectangular filters fit into a slotted holder. One holder and one set of filters can serve many lenses, each of which just needs a simple adaptor ring.

A few specialist lenses, including super-telephoto, extreme wide-angle, and fish-eye lenses, require equally specialist filters, fitting either at the rear of the lens or by a slot in the lens barrel.

› UV and skylight filters

Both of these filters cut out excess ultraviolet light, which can make images appear extremely blue. The skylight filter also has a slight warming effect. They also protect the front element of the lens.

› Polarizing filter

The polarizing filter cuts down reflections from most surfaces, intensifying colors in rocks and vegetation, for instance. It can make reflections on water and glass virtually disappear, restoring transparency. Rotating the filter strengthens or weakens its effect. The polarizer can also cut through atmospheric haze (though not mist or fog) like nothing else, and can make blue skies appear more intense. These effects are strongest when shooting at right angles to the sunlight, vanishing when the sun is directly behind or in front. When used with wide-angle lenses, the effect can vary conspicuously across the field of view. You might only use it occasionally, but some of its effects are virtually impossible to reproduce by any other means, even in post-processing. Sometimes it can be priceless.

› Neutral density filters

Neutral density (ND) filters reduce the amount of light reaching the lens, without shifting its color—hence "neutral". ND filters can be either plain or graduated.

POLAR EXPLORATION ❯❯
A polarizing filter can intensify colors and accentuate clouds (as seen in the right side of this composite image). *85mm, 1/250 sec. (left) and 1/80 sec., f/11, ISO 200.*

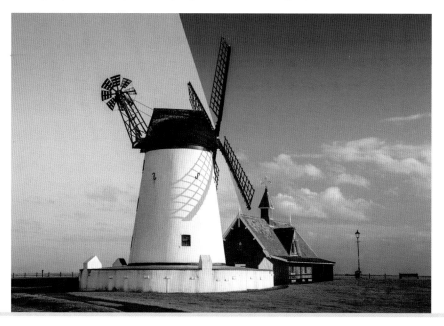

A plain ND filter allows you to set slower shutter speeds and/or wider apertures than otherwise possible. A classic example is shooting waterfalls, where you may want a long shutter speed to create a silky blur.

Graduated ND filters have neutral density over half their area, with the other half being clear, and a gradual transition in the center. They are widely used in landscape photography to compensate for wide differences in brightness between sky and land.

Tip

The effect of a graduated ND filter can be unpleasantly obvious, especially when the skyline is irregular, as in a mountain or city view. There are several alternative ways to deal with wide ranges of brightness, including Active D-Lighting (page 98) and HDR imaging (page 102).

› Special effects filters

Soft-focus filters are still used in portrait photography, but have been widely supplanted by digital post-processing. Much the same is true of the "starburst". Both of these can be replicated in-camera, using **Soft** and **Cross Screen** respectively in the **Filter effects** section of the Retouch menu (*page 129*).

"Effects" images were all the rage in the 1970s, when the Cokin system became available to stills photographers, but the appeal soon palled, although there's been a revival with the likes of Instagram. Just remember, if you capture the image "straight", and apply effects through the Retouch menu or in post-processing, you can always change your mind!

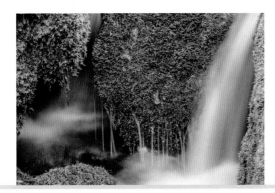

FALLING WATER 〈〈
A plain Neutral Density filter may be useful when you want to use really low shutter-speeds, for instance, to blur water. *70mm, 2 sec., f/22, ISO 100, tripod.*

» ESSENTIAL ACCESSORIES

EN-EL14a battery
Without a live battery, your D5300 is a useless deadweight. It's always wise to have a fully charged spare on hand—especially in cold conditions, when using the screen extensively, or when shooting movies. If you shoot movies seriously, make that "several fully charged spares". Older EN-EL14 batteries can also be used.

MH-24 charger
This is vital for keeping the battery fully charged and ready.

BF-1A/1B body cap
Protects the interior of the camera when no lens is attached.

Camera cases
Nikon don't supply a case, but unless the camera lives permanently indoors, one should be seen as essential. The most practical is a simple drop-in pouch which can be worn on a waist-belt. Excellent examples come from makers like Think Tank, Camera Care Systems, and LowePro.

If you want to carry a larger system, perhaps including several lenses, a flash, and a tripod, then a backpack-type bag is kindest on your spine.

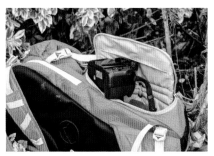

BACKPACK ≈
Backpacks are best for the spine when carrying heavy loads.

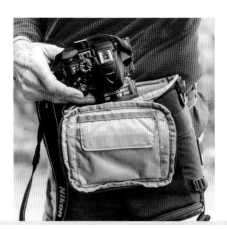

POUCH PROTECTION «
A padded pouch (this one's by Think Tank Photo) combines good protection and easy access.

8 » OPTIONAL ACCESSORIES

A selection from Nikon's extensive range is listed here.

AC Adapter EH-5b

Can be used to power the camera directly from the AC mains, allowing uninterrupted shooting in, for example, long studio sessions. (A Power Connector EP-5A is also required.)

ME-1 stereo microphone

Greatly improves sound quality in movie shooting (*see page 174*).

Diopter Adjustment

The D5300's Viewfinder has built-in dioptric adjustment (*see page 24*). If your eyesight is beyond its range, Nikon produces a series of Viewfinder lenses between −5 and +3 m^{-1}, with the designation DK-20C.

> ### Tip
>
> *It's usually easier to wear contact lenses or glasses. My prescription is around −5 m^{-1} and I've never had any problem using the D5300 while wearing contacts.*

Wireless remote control ML-L3

This inexpensive little infrared unit allows the camera to be triggered from a distance of up to 16ft (5m). There are receivers on both the front and rear of the camera, allowing operation from a wide range of positions.

Nikon's WR-R10 wireless transceiver and WR-T10 wireless transmitter offer a much wider range of functions, at a much higher price. Third-party units like Hahnel's Giga T Pro II can give you much of this power at a lower cost. However, none of these let you see what the camera is seeing, which Wi-Fi and a smartphone can give you (*see page 224*).

WIRELESS REMOTE CONTROL ML-L3 ⌄

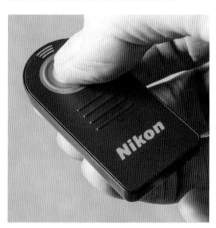

» CAMERA SUPPORT

Screen shades

Camera LCD screens can be impossible to see properly in bright sunlight. The Viewfinder is much better for shooting in bright light, but you can still need the screen for Live View and especially for shooting movies. Third-party companies produce accessory screen shades— probably the best-known name is Hoodman. However, if you only need one occasionally, you can improvise: I have heard of people using the cardboard core from a toilet roll.

There's much more to camera support than tripods, although these remain a staple, of course.

› Tripods

Vibration Reduction (VR) lenses, plus the D5300's ability to produce fine images at high ISO settings, do encourage handholding, but there are still many occasions when nothing replaces a tripod. While light weight and low cost always appeal, beware of tripods that simply aren't sturdy enough to provide decent support, especially with longer lenses. A good tripod is an investment that will last for years. The best combination of low weight with good rigidity comes (at a price) in titanium or carbon fiber. Carbon-fiber tripods are made by Manfrotto and Gitzo, among others. My first Manfrotto carbon tripod outlived several cameras and indeed took me from shooting film into the digital age.

When shooting movies, a tripod is essential, and many tripods are designed specifically for this purpose (*see page 176*).

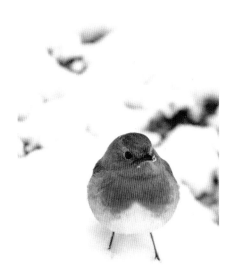

SHY SUBJECTS «
Backing away from the camera and firing the shutter remotely can be a good approach with shy subjects. *60mm, 1/80 sec., f/5, ISO 400.*

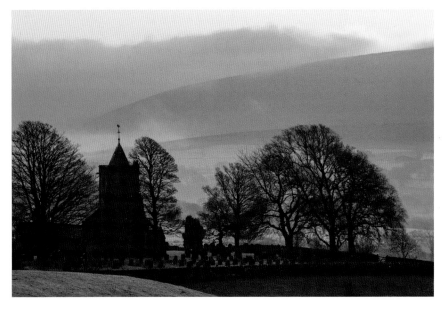

SOLID SUPPORT ⚲

Tripods are ideal for a wide variety of subjects.
100mm, 1/25 sec., f/11, ISO 100, tripod.

› Monopods

Monopods can't equal the ultimate stability
of a tripod, but are light, easy to carry, and
quick to set up. They are favored by sports
photographers, who often need to react
quickly to fast-moving events while using
hefty long telephoto lenses.

› Other camera support

There are many other solutions for camera
support, both proprietary products and
improvised alternatives. It's still hard to beat
the humble beanbag—these can be
home-made, or bought from various
suppliers. For movie-specific camera
support, *see page 176.*

» STORAGE

› Memory cards

The D5300 stores images on Secure Digital (SD), SDHC, and SDXC cards. On long trips it's easy to fill up even large-capacity memory cards and they are now remarkably cheap, so it's advisable to carry a spare or two.

Memory card performance is measured in two ways: speed rating or rated speed (e.g. 30MB/s) is the key measure when shooting stills, especially RAW files.

The other measure is class or speed class rating (e.g. Class 10), which is more important when shooting video.

› Portable storage devices

Memory cards rarely fail but it's always worth backing up valuable images as soon as possible. Many photographers use some sort of mobile device for backing up. Dedicated photo storage devices like the Vosonic VP8870 and Epson P7000 are increasingly hard to find, as most people (if they back up at all!) now use a laptop, smartphone, or tablet (*see page 224*).

› Card care

If a memory card is lost or damaged before downloading or backing up, your images are lost too. Blank cards are cheap but cards full of images are irreplaceable—unlike the camera itself. As SD cards use solid-state memory, they are pretty robust but it's still wise to treat them with care. Keep them in their original plastic cases, or something more substantial, and avoid exposure to extremes of temperature, direct sunlight, liquids, and strong electromagnetic fields.

> **Note:**
> There seems to be no evidence that modern airport X-ray machines have any harmful effect on either digital cameras or memory cards.

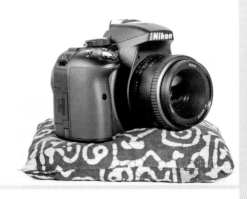

BEANBAG »
A simple home-made beanbag that has served me well for many years.

» CARE

The D5300 is robust, but it's also packed with complex and potentially delicate electronic and optical technology. A few simple precautions should help it keep functioning perfectly for many years.

› Basic care

Keeping the camera clean is fundamental. Keep the camera in a case when not in use. Remove dust and dirt with a blower, then wipe with a soft, dry cloth.

The rear screen may be tough enough to survive without a protective cover, but it will need cleaning periodically. Use a blower to remove loose dirt, then wipe the surface carefully with a clean, soft cloth or a swab designed for the purpose. Do not apply pressure and never use household cleaning fluids.

Warning!

Astonishingly, the *Nikon Reference Manual* (page 240) implies that the reflex mirror can be cleaned with a cloth and cleaning fluid. This flies in the face of normal advice: never touch the reflex mirror in any way, as it is extremely delicate. Remove dust from the mirror with gentle use of an air-blower, and nothing else.

› Cleaning the sensor

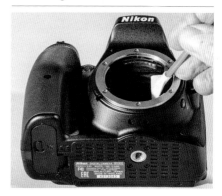

SENSOR CLEANING ⌃
Cleaning the sensor requires confidence—and great care!

While the D5300 dispenses with the optical low-pass filter over the sensor (*page 8*), there is still a protective filter in front of the sensor, and although everyone refers to "sensor cleaning", it's this filter, not the sensor itself, with which we are actually concerned. This filter can attract dust, which will appear as dark spots in your images. However careful you are, unless you never change lenses, some dust will find its way in. Fortunately, the D5300 has a self-cleaning facility. This can be activated manually at any time or set to occur automatically when the camera is switched on and/or off: select options using **Clean Image Sensor** in the Setup menu.

Occasionally, however, stubborn spots may remain and it may become necessary to clean the filter manually. This is best done in a clean, draught-free, and well-lit area, preferably using a lamp which can be aimed into the camera's interior.

Ensure the battery is fully charged: use a mains adapter if available. Remove the lens, switch the camera on, and select **Lock mirror up** for cleaning from the Setup menu. Press the shutter-release button to lock up the mirror. First, attempt to remove dust using a hand-blower (not compressed air or other aerosol). If this appears ineffective, consider using a dedicated sensor cleaning swab, carefully following its supplied instructions. Do not use other brushes or cloths and never touch the sensor with your finger. The result could be far worse than a few dust spots. When cleaning is complete, turn the camera off, and the mirror will reset.

Warning!

Any damage caused by heavy-handed manual cleaning or the use of inappropriate products could void your warranty. If in doubt, consult a professional dealer or camera repairer.

Tip

If (or rather, when) spots do appear on images, they can always be removed using, for example, the Clone tool or Healing brush in Adobe Photoshop. In Nikon Capture NX2 this process can be automated by creating a Dust-off reference image (see pages 123, 227). Spot-removal can be applied across batches of images in Adobe Lightroom.

WATER WHEELS ⮛
Care includes protecting the camera in difficult conditions. *200mm, 1/800 sec., f/4, ISO 800.*

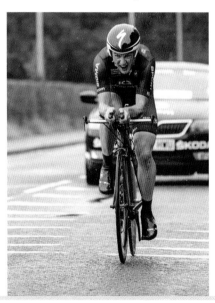

8 » BRAVING THE ELEMENTS

› Cold

Nikon specify an operating temperature range of 32–104°F (0–40°C). When ambient temperatures fall below freezing, the camera can still be used, but aim to keep it within the specified range as far as possible. Keeping the camera in an insulated case or under outer layers of clothing between shots will help keep it warmer than the surroundings. If it does become chilled, battery life can be severely reduced (carry a spare). In extreme cold, the LCD displays may become erratic or disappear completely and ultimately the camera may cease to function. If allowed to warm up gently, no permanent harm should result.

› Heat and humidity

Extremes of heat and humidity (Nikon stipulate over 85%) can be even more problematic, as they are more likely to lead to long-term damage. In particular, rapid transfers from cool environments to hot and humid ones (air-conditioned hotel to sultry streets) can cause internal condensation. If such transitions occur, pack the camera and lens(es) in airtight containers with sachets of silica gel, which will absorb any moisture. Allow equipment to reach ambient temperature before unpacking, let alone using, it.

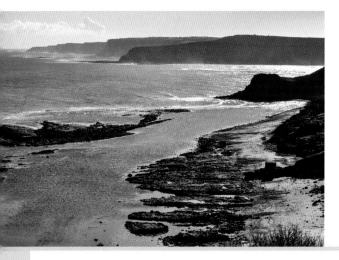

SPRAY **«**
A dramatic location but potentially hazardous for the camera: salt spray is notoriously insidious. Sand, dust, and dirt all require care too. *62mm, 1/1600 sec., f/9, ISO 320.*

› Water

The D5300 does not claim to be waterproof, but brief exposure to light rain is unlikely to do permanent harm. Keep exposure to a necessary minimum, and wipe regularly with a microfiber cloth (always handy to deal with accidental splashes). Avoid using the built-in flash and keep the hotshoe cover in place. Double-check that all access covers on the camera are properly closed.

Take extra care to avoid contact with salt water. If this does occur, clean carefully and immediately with a cloth lightly dampened with fresh and preferably distilled water.

Ideally, protect the camera with a waterproof cover. A simple plastic bag will provide rudimentary protection, but purpose-made rain-guards are available, such as the HydroPhobia from Think Tank.

Aquapac's reasonably-priced DSLR case is a good match for the D5300 and is rated for immersion at a depth of 33ft or 10m.

› Dust

To minimize ingress of dust into the camera, take great care when changing lenses. Aim the camera slightly downward and stand with your back to any wind. In really bad conditions (such as sandstorms) it's best not to change lenses at all, and better still to protect the camera with a waterproof, and therefore also dustproof, case. Dust that settles on the outside of the camera is relatively easy to remove; the safest way is with a hand-operated or compressed-air blower. Do this before changing lenses, memory cards, or batteries, keeping all covers closed until the camera is clean.

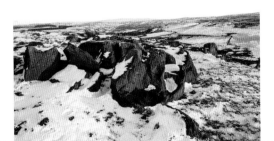

WINTER WONDERLAND　　**«**
Winter conditions offer wonderful photographic opportunities but can be challenging for cameras. *18mm, 1/40 sec., f/11, ISO 400.*

CONNECTION

In digital photography, connecting to external devices—especially computers—is not an optional extra: it's how you store, organize, backup, and print images. The D5300 is designed to facilitate these operations, and a couple of useful cables are included with the camera.

» CONNECTING TO A COMPUTER

Connecting to a Mac or PC allows you to store, organize, and backup your images. It also helps you exploit the full power of the D5300, including the ability to optimize image quality from RAW files. Some software packages allow "tethered" shooting, where images appear on the computer straight after capture; Nikon Camera Control Pro 2 (optional purchase) goes further, allowing the camera to be controlled directly from the Mac or PC.

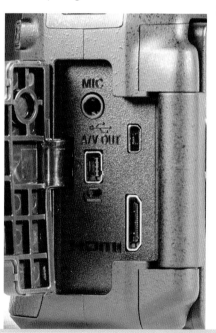

› Computer requirements

The large file sizes produced by the D5300 place extra demands on computer systems, stressing processor speed, hard disk capacity, and—above all—memory (RAM). Systems with less than 4GB of RAM may run slowly when dealing with RAW or full-size JPEG images from the camera. Fortunately, adding extra RAM to most systems is relatively easy and inexpensive. Extra hard disk space can also be helpful, as the system will slow significantly when the hard disk becomes close to capacity.

A CD drive is useful but not essential for installing the supplied Nikon View NX2

CONNECTION PORTS   «
The open cover on the left side of the D5300 reveals the connection ports.

software, as it can also be downloaded from the Nikon website. Nikon View NX2 requires one of the following operating systems: Mac OS X (Version 10.6.8, 10.7.5 or 10.8.5); Windows 8 (Pro/Enterprise); Windows 7 (Service Pack 1); Windows Vista (Service Pack 2); Windows XP (Service Pack 3).

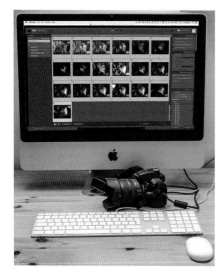

A D5300 CONNECTED TO A COMPUTER ⌃

› Backing up

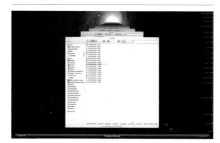

APPLE'S TIME MACHINE ⌃
Time Machine makes backing up easy.

Until they are backed up, your precious images exist solely as data on the camera's memory card. Memory cards are robust but not indestructible, and in any case you will surely wish to format and reuse them. However, when images are transferred to the computer and the card is formatted, those images once more exist in one single location—the computer's hard drive. If anything happens to that hard drive, whether fire, theft, or hardware failure, you could lose thousands of irreplaceable images. The simplest form of backup is to a second hard drive—the "gold standard" requires multiple drives, one of which is always kept off site. Online backup is also an option, but unless you shoot very sparingly you'll find free services offer nowhere near enough space. If you shoot a lot, paid services can easily cost more than a couple of spare hard drives.

› Color calibration

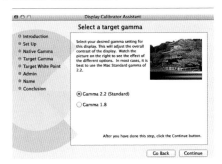

CALIBRATION SOFTWARE ⌃
The Display Calibrator Assistant included
with Mac OSX.

A major headache for digital camera users
is that images look one way on the camera
monitor, different on the computer screen,
different when you email them to your
friends, and different again when printed.
To achieve consistency across different
devices, it's vital above all that your main
computer screen is correctly set up and
calibrated. This may seem complex and
time-consuming but ultimately saves much
time and frustration. Detailed advice is
beyond the scope of this book but try
searching System Help for "monitor
calibration". There's more detail in the
Digital SLR Handbook (from this author
and publisher) and there's some useful
advice at http://www.cambridgeincolor.
com/color-management-printing.htm.

› Connecting the camera

The D5300's Wi-Fi connection is useful,
but doesn't let you transfer images directly
to a laptop or desktop. For this, unless you
use an Eye-Fi card (*see page 227*), you
need a physical connection. The camera
is supplied with a suitable USB cable. This
description is based on Nikon Transfer,
part of the supplied View NX2 package.
The procedure with other software will
be similar in outline but different in detail.

1) Start the computer and let it boot up.
Open the cover on the camera's left side
and insert the smaller end of the supplied
USB cable into the AV/USB slot; insert
the other end into a USB port on the
computer (not an unpowered hub or
port on the keyboard).

2) Switch on the camera. Nikon Transfer
starts automatically (unless you have
configured its Preferences not to do so).

3) The Nikon Transfer window offers
various options. The following are
particularly important.

4) To transfer selected images only, use the
check box below each thumbnail to select/
deselect as required.

5) Click the **Primary Destination** tab to
choose where photos will be stored. You

can create a new subfolder for each transfer, rename images as they are transferred, and so on.

6) Click the **Backup Destination** tab if you want Nikon Transfer to create backup copies automatically during transfer.

7) When transfer is complete, switch off the camera and disconnect the cable.

Tip

Most people find it more convenient to transfer photos by inserting the memory card into a card-reader. Many PCs have built-in SD card slots but separate card-readers are cheap and widely available. Older card-readers may not support SDHC or SDXC cards. The procedure is essentially the same.

If you transfer images using a card-reader, remove the card from the system like any other external drive when the download is finished. In Windows, use **Safely Remove Hardware**; in Mac OS X use **Command + E** or drag the D5300 icon to the Trash.

› Importing movies

The basic procedure for importing movies is the same as for still images. Nikon Transfer will recognize and import them, but you will probably want to store movies in a different folder to that for your still images. Often it's better to import movies through your editing software (*see page 181*); this ensures that all your movie clips are stored in the same place and that the software can immediately locate them for editing purposes.

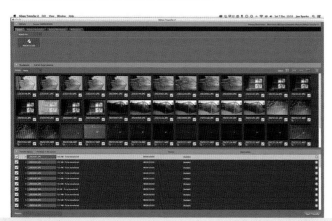

NIKON TRANSFER «

The D5300 is the first Nikon DSLR with onboard Wi-Fi. This will undoubtedly be welcome for many users, but it has to be said that its capabilities are strictly limited. First of all, the onboard Wi-Fi will only connect to mobile devices (iOS or Android); there appears to be no way to connect to a laptop or desktop computer. Secondly, the statement in the Nikon manual that you can "control the camera remotely" is distinctly optimistic—you can set focus and trigger the shutter, but can't change any other settings.

Unfortunately, there appears to be no way to control the camera remotely from a computer without a wired connection—the term "tethered shooting" seems all too apt. If you just want to transfer images to a computer over a wireless network, the obvious option is to use an Eye-Fi card.

› Setting up onboard Wi-Fi

To use onboard Wi-Fi with your iOS or Android device, first download Nikon's Wireless Mobile Utility from the App Store or Android Market.

To establish a connection
The process is described for an iOS device (iPhone or iPad); the process on Android or other mobile devices is basically similar but may require a few extra steps.

1) Go to the Wi-Fi item in the Setup menu. Select Wi-Fi and press ▶.

2) Select Network connection and press ▶.

3) Select Enable and press (OK).

4) On the iOS device, go to Settings and tap Wi-Fi.

5) Under Choose a Network, tap the network whose name begins "Nikon_".

The camera and device should now be connected and you can now go to the Wireless Mobile Utility (WMU) to take new photos or transfer existing shots to your device.

› Using Wireless Mobile Utility

The opening screen of the Utility has two main options: Take photos and View photos.

Taking photos
Before taking photos, make sure camera settings, including Live View focusing options (*page 90*) are as you want them.

1) Tap Take photos. The camera's mirror flips up and displays a Live View image.

2) If Live View AF-area mode is 🔲 Wide-area AF or 🔲 Normal area AF, you can focus by tapping the appropriate place on the iPhone or iPad screen. Unfortunately, you can't zoom the display to check focus even more precisely (although with iPads you get a preview that's significantly larger than the camera's screen, especially if you use the iPad in landscape orientation).

3) Tap the camera icon at the bottom of the screen (left side in landscape

NIKON WIRELESS MOBILE UTILITY ⌄
Taking photographs using a mobile device.

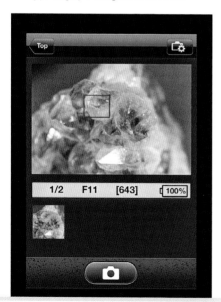

orientation) to take a photo. This will swiftly download to the device and a thumbnail appears in the "tray" below the Live View images (to the left in landscape orientation).

4) A simple way to finish shooting is to tap Top, which returns to the app's opening screen and ends Live View.

Viewing photos

1) In the opening screen, tap View photos. The options now are Pictures on D5300, Camera roll, and Latest downloads.

2) Tap Pictures on D5300 to see all photos on the camera. You can then select any of these you wish to transfer. Note, however, that NEF (RAW) files will be converted to JPEG on transfer.

3) Tap Camera roll to see images already on the device.

4) Tap Latest downloads to see shots recently taken with the D5300.

» SOFTWARE AND IMAGE PROCESSING

The D5300 is bundled with Nikon View NX2 software. This includes Nikon Transfer (see Connecting the camera, *page 222*). View NX2 itself covers most of the main processes: you can view and browse images, save them in other formats, and print. However, editing and enhancing images (including RAW files) is not very intuitive, compared to using iPhoto or Lightroom. Results might be technically superior, but achieving them might try your patience. It's also weak for organizing and cataloging images.

Using Nikon View NX2

1) From any browser view (e.g. thumbnail grid), click on an image to highlight it. Image Viewer shows the image larger, with a histogram, and there's also a Full Screen view.

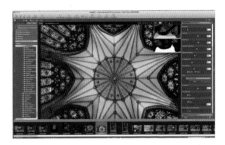

NIKON VIEW NX2   ☆

2) The Metadata tab gives detailed info about the image and the Adjustment palette allows adjustments such as exposure and white balance.

3) Close the image and you will be asked if you want to save any adjustments. You do not need to export the file immediately.

Nikon View NX2 file format options

JPEG	Choose compression ratio: Highest Quality; High Quality; Good Balance; Good Compression Ratio; Highest Compression Ratio.	Suitable if extensive further editing is not envisaged. For good quality prints choose High or Highest Quality.
TIFF (8-bit)		Creates larger file sizes than JPEG, without a noticeable gain in quality: 16-bit is advised for extensive retouching work.
TIFF (16-bit)		The best choice when further editing is anticipated.

4) To export the file as a TIFF or JPEG that can be viewed, edited, and printed by other applications, choose Convert Files from the File menu. You can resize and rename the image too.

5) The File Format menu in the Convert Files dialog offers three options (see the table on the previous page).

› Nikon Capture NX2

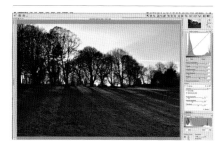

NIKON CAPTURE NX2 ⏫

For a wider range of editing options, especially in relation to RAW files, Nikon Capture NX2 (optional purchase) or one of its third-party rivals is essential. Unlike rivals such as Adobe Lightroom or Photoshop, Capture NX2 cannot open RAW files from non-Nikon cameras. Capture NX2 has a quirky interface; some love it, others just can't get on with it, and in any case you'll need another app for cataloging.

› Camera Control Pro 2

Camera Control Pro 2 is a professional product at a professional price, and allows you to control the D5300 directly from a Mac or PC ("tethered shooting"). As images are captured you can check them in detail on the large, color-corrected computer screen; Live View integration allows real-time viewing. It requires a physical connection.

› Eye-Fi

An Eye-Fi card looks and operates like a conventional SD memory card, but includes an antenna which allows it to connect to WiFi networks, allowing you to transfer images wirelessly. Some Eye-Fi cards also support ad-hoc networks, allowing images to be transferred to a laptop or iPad when out of the range of regular WiFi.

Eye-Fi software is installed by plugging the card into any WiFi-enabled Mac or PC; that computer becomes the default destination for Eye-Fi upload. The card can then be inserted in the camera; use **Eye-Fi Upload** in the Setup menu to enable transfers. When out of range of your network, turn Eye-Fi off to save battery power. The card still functions as a regular memory card.

The undisputed market leader is Adobe Photoshop. Its power is enormous—far beyond most users' needs. Adobe has recently changed to a subscription model under the Creative Cloud label, which means that the software is regularly updated (and version numbers don't mean very much any more)—but it will stop working if you don't keep up the subscription payments.

Many will prefer the far more affordable Photoshop Elements, which still has sophisticated editing features, including the ability to open RAW files from the D5300. It is currently still obtainable on the more familar model where you pay once for a perpetual licence to use the software.

Photoshop Elements includes an Organizer module, which allows you to "tag" photos, assign them to "Albums", or add keywords.

Mac users have another excellent choice in the form of iPhoto (latest version iPhoto 11), pre-installed on new Macs; like Photoshop Elements, it combines organizing and editing abilities. Unbeatable for ease of use, iPhoto can open RAW files from the D5300, but—unlike Photoshop Elements—cannot edit in 16-bit depth, which is recommended for best results.

Finally, there are two one-stop solutions in the shape of Apple's Aperture (Mac only) and Adobe Lightroom (Mac and PC).

Highly recommended if you regularly shoot RAW, both offer powerful organizing and cataloging, seamlessly integrated with advanced image editing. Editing is "non-destructive"—edit settings (any changes you make to your image, including color, cropping, and so on) are recorded alongside the original RAW (or DNG) file without creating a new TIFF or JPEG file. TIFF or JPEG versions, incorporating all the edits, can be exported as and when needed. Aperture is now very keenly priced and can be obtained at lower cost than Photoshop Elements, yet is significantly more powerful.

Recent versions of Aperture and Lightroom both support tethered shooting, as do several other apps; Mac users have a fine free option in the shape of Sofortbild.

> **Note:**
> Older versions of Photoshop, Elements, and Lightroom will not recognize RAW files created by the D5300. One workaround is to use Adobe DNG Converter (free) to convert files to the widely compatible DNG format. However, this adds an extra, time-consuming, step to your workflow. Upgrading Lightroom or Photoshop Elements is an easier, and reasonably affordable, solution.

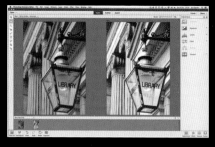

ADOBE PHOTOSHOP ELEMENTS «
The "before" and "after" views in
Quick Edit mode.

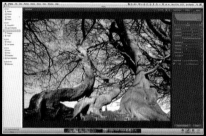

IPHOTO'S ADJUST PALETTE «
Quick and flexible image editing.

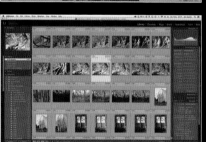

ADOBE LIGHTROOM'S LIBRARY MODULE «
Powerful tool for organizing your images.

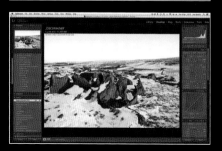

ADOBE LIGHTROOM'S DEVELOP MODULE «
The Develop module offers a very wide
spectrum of RAW adjustments.

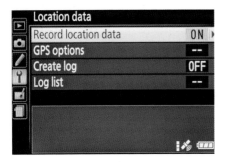

The D5300 is the first Nikon DSLR with onboard GPS. This function is becoming common on compact cameras and is almost a given with smartphones, but still relatively rare in DSLRs. The attractions of being able to record the location where every photo was taken will be obvious to many users, but using the GPS does have an impact on battery life. This could be a particular issue when travelling or trekking—but of course these are just the times when recording GPS location data could be most valuable.

The GPS receiver is **Off** by default—enable it via the **Location data** item in the Setup menu. This item also contains a few important options.

Standby timer is important in relation to battery life. If set to **OFF**, it stops the meters turning off and returning the camera to standby. This ensures that the GPS receiver is always able to connect to the satellite network (unless the signal is

blocked). If you select **On**, the meters will turn off after 1 minute. This saves battery power, but next time you take a picture the GPS receiver may not have time to get a fix, in which case no location data will be recorded.

There's also an option to **Set clock from satellite**. As the GPS network embodies some of the most accurate timing in existence, this should mean that your camera clock is always bang on.

Another option is **Update A-GPS data**. Assisted GPS (A-GPS) files can help the receiver acquire a location fix more quickly. This is worth considering if you are a serious GPS user, but A-GPS files are time-limited and need to be renewed every couple of weeks, so you might conclude that it's more trouble than it's worth.

Finally, there's an option to **Create log**, which lets the camera record its position regularly, giving you a record of your movements while using the camera. However, bear in mind that this is another drain on the battery.

» CONNECTING TO A PRINTER

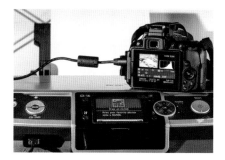

A D5300 CONNECTED TO A PRINTER ⌃

The camera's memory card can be inserted into a compatible printer or taken to a photo printing store. Alternatively, the camera can be connected to any printer that supports the PictBridge standard.

However, for maximum flexibility and power when printing, transfer photographs to a computer first.

Tip

*RAW images can't be printed directly from the camera, but you can use the **NEF (RAW) processing** item in Retouch menu (page 131) to create a JPEG copy for direct printing.*

To connect to a printer
1) Turn the camera off.

2) Turn the printer on and connect the supplied USB cable. Insert the the smaller end of the cable into the USB slot, under the cover on the left side of the camera.

3) Turn the camera on. You should now see a welcome screen, followed by a PictBridge playback display. There's now a choice between **Printing pictures one at a time** or **Printing multiple pictures**.

Printing pictures one at a time
1) Select the photo you wish to print, then press ⊙⊛. This reveals a menu of printing options—see the table on the next page. Use the Multi-selector to navigate the menu and highlight specific options; press ⊙⊛ to select.

2) When the required options have been set, select **Start printing** and press ⊙⊛. To cancel at any time, press ⊙⊛ again.

Printing options

Option name	Options available	Notes
Page size		Options depend on paper sizes the printer can support.
No. of copies	1–99	Use ▲/▼ to choose number, then press ⓞⓚ to select.
Border	Printer default Print with border No border	If **Print with border** is selected, borders will be white.
Time stamp	Printer default Print time stamp No time stamp	Prints time and date when image was taken.
Crop	Crop No cropping	**Crop** prints selected area only to size selected under **Page size**. Screen shows image with border delineating crop area. Use ⊖ and ⊕ to change size of this area; use Multi-selector to reposition it. When satisfied, press ⓞⓚ.

› Printing multiple pictures

You can print several pictures at once. You can also create an index print of all JPEG images (up to a maximum of 256) currently stored on the memory card.

NEF (RAW) images cannot be printed. With the PictBridge menu displayed, press ⓞⓚ. The following options are displayed.

Print Select	Use the Multi-selector to scroll through pictures on the memory card. To choose currently selected image for printing, press ▲. The picture is marked 凸 and number of prints set to 1. Press ▲ repeatedly to print more copies. Repeat to select further images and choose number of prints from each. Finally, press ⓞⓚ to display PictBridge menu and select printing options, as in table above. Select Start printing and press ⓞⓚ.
Select date	Prints one copy of each picture taken on selected date(s).
Print (DPOF)	Prints images already selected using **Print set (DPOF)** option in Playback Menu (*see page 109*).
Index Print	Prints all JPEG images on the memory card, up to maximum of 256. If more images exist, only the first 256 will be printed.

» CONNECTING TO A TV

You can playback photos and movie clips through both standard TVs and HDMI (High Definition Multimedia Interface) sets. They require different cables, but in other respects the process is essentially the same. An AV cable is supplied with the camera.

1) Check that the camera is set to the correct mode in the Setup menu (**NTSC** or **PAL** for standard TVs and VCRs, or **HDMI**, *see page 125*).

2) Turn the camera off. Important: always do this before connecting or disconnecting the cable. ·

3) Open the cover on the left side of the camera and insert the cable into the appropriate slot (AV-out or HDMI). Connect the other end to the TV.

4) Tune the TV to a video or HDMI channel.

5) Turn the camera on and press the playback button. Images remain visible on the camera monitor as well as on the TV and you navigate using the Multi-selector in the usual way. The Slide show item in the Playback menu (*page 109*) can be used to automate playback.

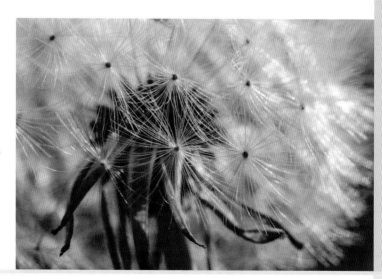

DANDELION »
Specialist macro lenses are essential for capturing sharp close-up shots. *50mm macro, 1/400 sec., f/8, ISO 200.*

9 ›› GLOSSARY

8-bit, 12-bit, 16-bit *See* Bit depth.

Accessory shoe *See* Hotshoe.

Aperture The lens opening which admits light. Relative aperture sizes are expressed in f-numbers (see below).

Artefact Occurs when data or data produced by the sensor is interpreted incorrectly, resulting in visible flaws in the image.

Bit depth The amount of information recorded for each color channel. 8-bit, for example, means that the data distinguishes 28 or 256 levels of brightness for each channel. 16-bit images recognize over 65,000 levels per channel, which allows greater freedom in editing. The D5300 records RAW images in 12- or 14-bit depth and they are converted to 16-bit on import to the computer.

Bracketing Taking a number of otherwise identical shots in which just one parameter (e.g. exposure) is varied.

Buffer On-board memory that holds images until they can be written to the memory card.

Burst A number of frames shot in quick succession. The maximum burst size is limited by buffer capacity.

Channel The D5300, like other digital devices, records data for three separate color channels. *See* RGB.

Chimping Checking images on the screen after shooting.

CCD (charge-coupled device) A type of image sensor used in many digital cameras.

Class (or speed class) rating A measure of the performance of memory cards. Class rating is most important when shooting video. *See also* Speed rating.

Clipping Complete loss of detail in highlight or shadow areas of the image (sometimes both), leaving them as blank white or black.

CMOS (Complementary Metal Oxide Semiconductor) A type of image sensor used in many digital cameras, including the D5300.

Color temperature The color of light, expressed in degrees Kelvin (K). Confusingly, "cool" (bluer) light has a higher color temperature than "warm" (red) light.

CPU (Central Processing Unit) A small computer in the camera (also found in many lenses) that controls most or all of the unit's functions.

Crop factor *See* Focal length multiplication factor.

Diopter Unit expressing the power of a lens.

dpi (dots per inch) A measure of resolution: should strictly be applied only to printers. *See also* ppi.

Dynamic range The range of brightness from shadows to highlights within which the camera can record detail.

Exposure Used in several senses. For instance, "an exposure" is virtually synonymous with "an image" or "a photo": to make an exposure = to take a picture. Exposure also refers to the amount of light hitting the image sensor, and to systems for measuring this. *See also* Overexposure, Underexposure.

Ev (Exposure value) A standardized unit of exposure. 1 Ev halves or doubles the amount of light and is equivalent to 1 "stop" in traditional photographic parlance.

Extension rings/Extension tubes Hollow tubes which fit between the camera tube and lens, used to allow greater magnifications.

f-number Lens aperture expressed as a fraction of focal length; f/2 is a wide aperture and f/16 is narrow.

Fast (lens) Lens with a wide maximum aperture, e.g. f1.8. f/4 is relatively fast for long telephotos.

Fill-in flash Flash used in combination with daylight. Used with naturally backlit or harshly side-lit subjects to prevent dark shadows.

Filter A piece of glass or plastic placed in front of, within, or behind the lens to modify light.

Firmware Software which controls the camera. Updates are issued by Nikon from time to time and can be transferred to the camera via a memory card.

Focal length The distance (in mm) from the optical center of a lens to the point at which light is focused.

Focal length multiplication factor Because the D5300's sensor is smaller than a frame of 35mm film, the effective focal length of all lenses is multiplied by a factor of 1.5.

fps (frames per second) The number of exposures (photographs) that can be taken in a second. The D5300's maximum rate is 6fps.

Highlights The brightest areas of the scene and/or the image.

Histogram A graph representing the distribution of tones in an image, ranging from pure black to pure white.

ISO (International Standards Organization) ISO ratings express film speed and the sensitivity of digital sensors is quoted as ISO-equivalent.

JPEG (Joint Photographic Experts Group) A compressed image file standard. High levels of JPEG compression can reduce files to about 5% of their original size, but there may be some loss of quality.

LCD (Liquid crystal display) Flat screen, such as the D5300's rear monitor.

Macro A term used to describe close focusing and the close-focusing ability of a lens. A true macro lens has a reproduction ratio of 1:1 or better.

Megapixel *See* Pixel.

Noise Image interference manifested as random variations in pixel brightness and/or color.

Overexposure When too much light reaches the sensor, resulting in a too-bright image, often with clipped highlights.

Pixel (picture element) The individual colored dots (usually square) which make up a digital image. One million pixels = 1 megapixel.

Post-processing Adjustment to images on computer after shooting. Can cover anything from minor tweaks of brightness or color to extensive editing.

ppi (pixels per inch) Should be applied to digital files rather than the commonly used dpi.

Reproduction ratio The ratio between the real size of an object and the size of its image on the sensor.

Resolution The number of pixels for a given dimension, for example 300 pixels per inch. Resolution is often confused with image size. The native size of an image from the D5300 is 6000 x 4000 pixels; this could make a large but coarse print at 100 dpi or a smaller, finer one at 300 dpi.

RGB (red, green, blue) Digital devices, including the D5300, record color in terms of brightness levels of the three primary colors.

Sensor The light-sensitive image-forming chip at the heart of every digital camera.

Shutter The mechanism which controls the amount of light reaching the sensor by opening and closing to expose the sensor when the shutter-release button is pushed.

Speed rating/rated speed A measure of the performance of memory cards. Speed rating is most important when shooting still images. *See also* Class rating.

Speedlight Nikon's range of dedicated external flashguns.

Spot metering A metering system which takes its reading from the light reflected by a small portion of the scene.

Telephoto lens A lens with a large focal length and a narrow angle of view.

TIFF (Tagged Image File Format) A universal file format supported by virtually all image-editing applications.

TTL (through the lens) The viewing and metering of SLR cameras such as the D5300.

Underexposure When insufficient light reaches the sensor, resulting in a too-dark image, often with clipped shadows.

USB (Universal Serial Bus) A data transfer standard, used to connect to a computer.

Viewfinder An optical system used for framing the image. On an SLR camera such as the D5300 it shows the view as seen through the lens.

White balance A function which compensates for different color temperatures so that images may be recorded with correct color balance.

Wide-angle lens A lens with a short focal length and a wide angle of view.

Zoom A lens with variable focal length, giving a range of viewing angles. To zoom in is to change focal length to give a narrower view and zoom out is the converse. Optical zoom refers to the genuine zoom ability of a lens; digital zoom is the cropping of part of an image to produce an illusion of the same effect.

» USEFUL WEB SITES

NIKON-RELATED SITES

Nikon Worldwide
Home page for the Nikon Corporation
www.nikon.com

Nikon UK
Home page for Nikon UK
www.nikon.co.uk

Nikon USA
Home page for Nikon USA
www.nikonusa.com

Nikon User Support
European Technical Support Gateway
www.europe-nikon.comsupport

Nikon Info
User forum, gallery, news, and reviews
www.nikoninfo.com

Nikon Historical Society
Worldwide site for study of Nikon products
www.nikonhs.org

Nikon Links
Links to many Nikon-related sites
www.nikonlinks.com

Grays of Westminster
Legendary Nikon-only dealer (London)
www.graysofwestminster.couk

GENERAL SITES

Digital Photography Review
Independent news and reviews
www.dpreview.com

Thom Hogan
Real-world reviews and advice
www.dslrbodies.com

Jon Sparks
Landscape and outdoor pursuit
photography
www.jon-sparks.co.uk

EQUIPMENT

Adobe
Photoshop, Photoshop Elements, Lightroom
www.adobe.com

Apple
Aperture and iPhoto
www.apple.com

Aquapac
Waterproof cases
www.aquapac.net

Sigma
Independent lenses and flash units
www.sigma-imaging-uk.com

PHOTOGRAPHY PUBLICATIONS

Ammonite Press
Photography books
www.ammonitepress.com

**Black & White Photography magazine,
Outdoor Photography magazine**
www.thegmcgroup.com

» INDEX